A GUIDE TO CHANNELING

AND CHANNELED MATERIAL

by Theodore

transcribed by Lily Andrews

Cassandra Press

San Rafael, Ca. 94915

Cassandra Press
P.O. Box 868
San Rafael, Ca. 94915

Printed in the United States of America.

First printing 1990

ISBN 0-945946-10-4

Library of Congress Catalogue Card Number

90-81600

TABLE OF CONTENTS

I. WHAT IS CHANNELING?

What It Is— The Astral Plane and Its Inhabitants— The Causal Plane and Its Inhabitants— Capabilities and Limitations of Astral and Causal Beings— How to Handle Lower Astral Beings— Favorite Con Games of the Discarnate

II. WHO CAN CHANNEL?

Channeling and Evolution— The Lessons of the Old Cycle— How Do You Know You Are Ready to Be a Channel?— The Stages of Development— Lessons Faced by Mediums— Benefits to the Medium— Full Trance vs. Partial Trance

III. WHY CHANNEL?

The Wrong Reasons for Channeling— The Dangers of Asking Personal Questions— Obtaining Information About Others— Obtaining Information About Money Schemes— Beneficial Uses of Channeling— The Dangers of Channeling— The Dangers of the Ouija Board and Automatic Writing

IV. HOW TO CHANNEL

When Does It Start?— Is It Your Life Work?— Before Becoming a Professional Channel— How to Begin Your Work as a Professional— Being a Professional Channel— Preparations and Procedures for Channeling— Truth About Grounding— The Medium's Health

V. THE SESSION

The Client's Responsibilities— Evaluating the Channel and the Material— Warning Signs— Education and Licensing of Channels— Formulating Your Questions— Asking About Past Lives and the Future— Fruitful Areas of Inquiry— What to Do with the Information after the Reading— A Sample Session

PREFACE

I came to write this book, because it needed to be written—or rather I needed to write it. I struggled with channeling for sometime in my own development, and I felt the need to share with others not only what I learned but what, perhaps, still remained to be learned. When Theodore suggested we write this book, the idea resonated not only with my desire to share information with others but my own need for clarification on this subject.

With misinformation and confusion abounding these days about channeling, a clear understanding of it is difficult to find. In allowing Theodore to explain this subject from his point of view, I hoped to at least gather information from this source and label it as such. This does not mean, of course, that this information is absolute truth any more than information from any other source is. You must be the judge of its usefulness and validity for yourself, just as I have. I found it to be an accurate depiction of channeling as I understand it. Please take what is useful to you and utilize it for good. Any information that you choose to believe should be tested. Examine it within the context of your life and feel its truth within you. The ultimate test of its validity lies with you, but we must begin somewhere in seeking understanding, and I felt writing this to be a good place to start.

Today the mention of channeling or channeled information often evokes ridicule, jokes, or whispers. When this is no longer the case, we will know that something has changed. Whether we realize it or not, the fact is that there is much information in the world today that has come to us via channeling which has not only gained acceptance but forms a foundation for many of our perceptions. The democratic principles of our founding fathers are an example of this. Our future will be shaped to an even larger extent by information—scientific, technological, philosophical, and medical—that is being channeled today. The earth has finally reached a level in its development when information of this nature is more readily received and utilized.

Of course, along with this come the pitfalls of this kind of communication. During these times, we will not only gain in understanding and new ideas, but in our ability to discriminate and use this material wisely. We, as a group, will go through some of the stages mentioned in this book in developing greater wisdom and discrimination in the use of channeled material. This means that sometimes we will make mistakes in accepting and utilizing what is received. Because this may happen, however, is no reason to avoid information offered from these realms. But it does mean that we must carefully examine and cautiously apply whatever information we do receive, just as we do when it comes from other sources. These times are very exciting in this respect, and I welcome the opportunity to be part of this learning process and the continuing birth of new information.

I did not come to be doing what I am by an easy route, but maybe no one's route is particularly easy. Although I had always been a seeker, I never had had any unusual experiences in my life. I had no psychic experiences as a child, but I would have liked to have had them. This desire for psychic experiences was a problem for me, because in seeking them, I—like so many others—was seeking to be special in this way.

When I was told in a channeled reading that I would someday be able to reach the same level of reality with which I was speaking, I was not sure what that meant. Just to cover all the possibilities, I bought myself a ouija board, because the channel I consulted with, although a very reputable channel, had used one as an aide (she has not used one for many years now). This was, perhaps, my first mistake. But not knowing any better, I attempted to use the board every now and then alone, as I had seen her do. I did not have success with this until years later when I pulled it out and—low and behold!—it began to work for me. Within hours of that moment I no longer needed the ouija board because the words were coming through fast and furiously in my head. I was overwhelmed by this new-found ability and figured that, at last, I had access to all of the answers and that my life would never be the same. It is true that my life would never be the same but not in the way that I had hoped.

I had hoped to be relieved of the need to be human, relieved of the need to live with the uncertainties that we all live with as human beings. I had also hoped to finally get the attention and acclaim I desired. I got attention all right, only because I drew it to myself, but I didn't get any acclaim. The way I approached this subject with my friends was so egocentric and foolish that all I received was reproach. My ego was making a terrible fool of myself, and I could not seem to see what was happening or break myself loose from it. For an entire year, my experience with channeling was a little like being on a wild roller coaster ride and not being able to get off until it was over. When it was done, I came away with a new outlook on channeling and its dangers, because I had experienced them all. I was devastated by what I had experienced. I decided that I was not ready to channel and that if channeling held a positive purpose in my life besides teaching me what I had already painfully learned, it would come about not by me pursuing it but by it pursuing me. Therefore, I set aside this aspect of my life and went about living my life as the ordinary human being that I (at times, regretfully!) am.

I spent the next two years attending to my personal and spiritual growth through meditation and other spiritual work. But equally important, I immersed myself in the ordinary tasks of life—cleaning, cooking, shopping—and falling in love, for it was then that I met my husband. I was also working as an astrologer along with doing more conventional types of counseling, and I noticed that the level at which I was practicing astrology began to shift. No longer was I relying on the individual chart symbols to describe the person. I began to *feel* the energy of the chart and the level at which the symbols were operating. For me the chart became a clear and distinct story about the person rather than the maze of symbols it had been in the past.

As a means for redefining my understanding of astrology, I began to write about my new insights. At one point during my writing, an entity who introduced themselves as Theodore asked permission to speak with me. Being a conscious channel, this is not particularly difficult to do. And since I was feeling very centered in myself and no longer easily impressed by this kind of communication, I decided to allow this. What they had to offer was information concerning the relationship between past lives and the chart. Because I felt comfortable with my sense of this entity and with my ability to judge the value and validity of the information, I continued the dialogue. This was the beginning of a very fruitful and positive relationship with Theodore. We have since then collaborated on several books. The significant point here is that until my intuition developed fully, I was not in a position to discriminate clearly. I have allowed the material in this book and in others to come through me only because it fits intuitively with my own understanding of truth.

I can say now that I am grateful for my earlier trials with channeling, because these experiences prepared me like nothing else could have to continue on with this work and approach it with appropriate caution and humility. Having said this, I wish you well in your own exploration.

INTRODUCTION

We, the author of this book, are a non-physical entity who resides on the mid-causal plane. We have written this book for those who have some channeling ability and for those who want to understand this phenomenon in order to better evaluate its usefulness in their lives. Its purpose is not to crusade for channeling. On the contrary, many will feel it is less supportive of channeling than such a book should be. Rather, we hope it will serve as a resource that will enhance the public's understanding of what channeling is, who can do it, how it is useful, and how it can hinder one's growth.

Particular care has been taken to address those who have some channeling ability but who are not as yet developed to use it reliably for themselves and others. The ability to discriminate does not develop until one has reached a certain level in one's spiritual growth. The fact that many are able to channel but have not as yet reached this level is cause for much of the confusion and misinformation that abounds. As a consequence, channeling's reputation has suffered.

One of our goals in writing this is to affect the quality of what is allowed to be made public by establishing guidelines for evaluating channeled material and assisting those in the developing phase so that they can proceed in their development without causing trouble for themselves or others. Along these same lines, we also hope to promote credentialing or some means of evaluating the services of a channel. Some of the points that will be made can also be applied to psychics, as well as others who work intuitively with these subtle realms. At the same time, we hope to allay some of the fears and banish the superstitions regarding other forms of intelligence and the realms that lie beyond the five senses.

We are grateful for this opportunity to convey this information to you, for we feel it is very timely and sorely needed.

CHAPTER I

WHAT IS CHANNELING?

Channeling is the means by which information is conveyed from a non-physical reality to a physical reality. Clairaudience is another name for this ability. It is accomplished through an individual, called a channel or a medium, who has this special capability. There are different kinds of channels or mediums, but each has a nervous system that can receive auditory-like impressions.

The impressions come in the form of words in the language of the individual, although languages unknown to the channel have at times been used. The impressions are similar to thoughts. The difference is that the words are received rather than "thought about." Although the experienced channel can easily distinguish between thoughts and channeled words, the beginning channel has much more difficulty with this. There are those who superimpose words onto their own intuitive impressions and call this channeling; if one has not ever truly channeled, it is easy enough to assume that one is doing so when this labeling of intuitive impressions occurs.

True channeling occurs when the mind is still and receptive, allowing those from other levels to convey their concepts to the channel through his or her language. The concepts are translated into language with the help of the channel by using the channel's language system and background of knowledge. The entity conveying the information uses the language system and vocabulary of the channel, although words unknown to the channel may be used from time to time. In general, the channel needs some language base for the concepts that are being presented for the information to be conveyed properly. Otherwise, concepts will be put into language that does not fit, and misunderstandings will arise. This is one reason for misunderstandings about other realms of existence and about the workings of the universe; your language and current concepts do not contain the concepts the entity is attempting to convey. Thus God becomes an old gentleman overlooking the earth from a cloud, and Jesus becomes someone who washes away sins.

The more educated the channel is about the subject being conveyed, the easier it is to bring forth the information accurately. It is very difficult, for instance, for a channel to deliver complex scientific, technological, or mathematical information without a matching knowledge base. Thus even very developed channels or mediums may be unable to convey highly specialized concepts if their understanding of the subject is limited. It is for this reason that those seeking to convey specialized information should seek out a medium who has an understanding of the material. Because mediums are fairly rare and their knowledge bases may be limited, there is much information of use to humanity that is waiting to be conveyed.

The purpose of conveying information from other realities or realms is to enlighten and inform those on this plane of existence. Unfortunately, there are beings who are not so enlightened and who may interfere with this process and seek to deliver information that is less than accurate or helpful. Let us begin by looking into the various kinds of beings that exist beyond the physical realm as a way of understanding these realms and some of the pitfalls of channeling.

Most people are familiar with the concept of speaking to individuals who have died through what is known as seances. It is true that some mediums do perform this function reliably. It is also true that there are many who do not. It is difficult for the unsuspecting and vulnerable individual to discern who is fraudulent.

Generally, those who have died need to come to grips with their death without interference from those who remain on earth. Those who remain on earth need to accept the death of their loved ones and move on with their own lives. Although there are times when addressing those who have passed over may serve a positive purpose, it can hinder the progress of parties in both realms, especially in the case of those recently deceased. It is often best to leave this form of mediumship for only very special circumstances.

Besides those who have died recently and need to be allowed their own adjustment period and growth, are those who have died less recently. The same can be said for these individuals, although they will not always agree with you about this. They must be allowed— and encouraged— to continue their respective duties on the level of existence they inhabit. Many are discontent with their lot and wish to return to earth, but are not as yet allowed to do so for various reasons. Some are awaiting a proper re-entry time, some need to accomplish some learning before moving on, and some are simply awaiting the first available opportunity.

There are certain goals and lessons to be accomplished by these individuals just as there are for those who have just died, those who are currently living, and those like ourselves who inhabit slightly different planes. Many of those who are awaiting rebirth are doing so with great longing for life on earth. Communication with those on earth is extremely attractive to them, and some will use the opportunity to communicate as a means to avoid the tasks at hand. Many of the interactions that occur as a result of the ouija board are interactions of this nature. They occur because an individual on earth has opened himself or herself up to communication with these levels, and those who are tempted to respond will do so. It is highly unlikely that information received under these circumstances will be reliable. For one thing, the beings at this level do not have access to the kind of information human beings think they do; for another, there are many who simply enjoy playing with humans by providing inaccurate information.

There are two categories of beings on this level of existence who seek to communicate with the living: those who do not seek to harm, but who dispense inaccurate information, because they will not admit to not knowing something; and those who intentionally seek to harm by providing inaccurate information. The souls awaiting rebirth are of varying degrees of evolvement. Those who are more evolved on this level will be attending to what they are there to accomplish. Usually, only souls who are very young or who have been traumatized by death seek to communicate with those still on earth. Although there are a few evolved souls who fashion themselves as guides to avoid their immediate lessons, for the most part, the souls who seek to communicate with human beings are desperate and young. Young souls have developed little empathy, and this is even truer once they are out of the body. Thus it is not surprising to find actual cases of individuals seeking to harm or to have fun with those on earth.

It is important to understand that these souls have no capability of harming those on earth if those on earth do not take their advise or make decisions based on their information. Those on this level can only harm with words, and words are only harmful if the one receiving then allows these words to influence them to make choices they would not ordinarily make. Ideas about possession, ghosts, evil spirits, and the Devil come from experiences from this level. Much of what is commonly believed about these things is superstition and not fact. The superstitions held about evil spirits, ghosts, possession, and so forth are food for those who wish to play with the living. They use these beliefs to instill fear and awe. The greatest misconception is that these individuals are powerful— they are anything but that. However, your belief that they are powerful gives them power to control you through fear.

It is best to avoid speaking to beings who exist within the reality that awaits rebirth to avoid inaccurate information and interference in their growth. What makes dealing with this level of reality so precarious is that on occasion one may obtain information that happens to be true. The overall lesson learned by one's experience with this level is that each piece of information received must be evaluated; one must not assume that because one thing from a source was true, all information from this source is therefore true. This goes for those inhabiting our plane of existence as well, for information offered must be taken with the understanding that it may or may not be true. The difference between our level and this level is that we do have access to certain kinds of information, information is not offered unless some degree of accuracy exists, and information is not offered at all that is deemed to be unhelpful to the individual's growth.

This brings us to the next level of existence: those who no longer have a need to reincarnate in a physical body and who exist on a plane beyond those who await reincarnation. These are the souls who are waiting to reunite with others— called entity mates— who, when reunited, make up the next form of consciousness called an entity. These souls reside on what are known as the mid and higher astral planes. The difference between the mid and higher astral planes is in the work that is accomplished by those who reside there. Those on the mid-astral plane are making preparations to proceed to the higher astral, while those on the higher astral are free to engage in work to assist those on earth. These are the souls known as guides, who are called upon by most mediums for advice and information, although there are mediums who specialize in contacting those who are still participating in reincarnation. For the most part, mediums who are able to reach this level of intelligence and beyond are more highly developed in their abilities than mediums who can only contact those on the lower astral. More will be said about this later.

There are many kinds of guides residing on the higher astral. The most common kind are those whose main function is to act as a personal guide for one or more individuals. These guides are also called spirit helpers, spirit guides, or guardian angels. Most guides are able to monitor more than one individual at a time, although when one is learning this work, just one individual will be worked with at a time. The work of guides is to assist in conveying the intentions of the Higher Self to the individual. They act as conduits or amplifiers to the Higher Self, allowing an individual to be more readily in contact with the Higher Self. This may seem a ludicrous idea— why is this even necessary?

The answer lies in understanding that until one has reached a certain level in development, access to the Higher Self through one's native intuition is simply not possible. It is only later on in one's evolution that the intuition develops and one is able to intuit the intentions of the Higher Self. Thus these personal guides act to facilitate the accomplishment of the soul's Plan by assisting those with whom they are in contact to understand the Plan in a way that seemed intuitive but is not exactly so. When the intuition begins to develop, the role of the guide changes to that of an advisor, delivering guidance on specifics in the life through the intuition. Life is far easier for an individual once he or she reaches this level because of the availability of this guidance.

Intuition is frequently confused with insight. Insight is a far more intellectual process than intuition, which functions largely on levels of the unconscious. Insight comes from wisdom gained by experience and from learning acquired from training or vicarious means such as books. Insight is something that develops over lifetimes, as does intuition, but it comes from learning rather than from unconscious processes.

Intuition is the result of interaction between the unconscious and one's Higher Self. The Higher Self speaks to the individual through his or her unconscious in the form of intuition. When the individual is not highly developed, intuition is experienced as vague sensations and feelings, which may be given meaning by the intellect. When the intellect is involved in this way, the opportunity for misrepresentation is great. As the individual evolves, he or she learns to differentiate between intuition and thoughts, the intuitions become stronger in their sensations, and a sense of knowing rather than an intellectual response occurs. The sense of knowing is what we call intuition, and when it has developed to this level, it can usually be trusted. When intuition is developed to an extraordinary degree, the individual is said to be psychic. At some point during this development, some individuals are able to converse with the guides who have been working with them on an intuitive level. This is called channeling.

Most individuals have a number of guides of different kinds working with them at any one time. The particular guides that are working with them may change over the course of a lifetime except one, whom we will call the spirit guide, who is usually present throughout the entire lifetime. The spirit guide oversees the entire unfolding of the Plan in the individual's life. He (for lack of a better word) is responsible for calling forth others to assist in the Plan's unfolding. He notifies those guides who will work with the individual later in life when that time has arrived, and he consults with his own guides and others concerning the Plan of the individual he is guiding. He makes it his business to know every coming and going of the individual, every thought, and every turn of event. He will look in on the development of other individuals involved or soon to be involved in the individual's Plan, and he will work to facilitate the roles they play in the individual's life.

The spirit guide, and all others working with the individual, communicate the Plan through the process of intuition via the unconscious of the individual. One means by which this is accomplished is through dreams. Art and music are unconscious means sometimes used by guides to communicate as well. Another means of facilitating the Plan is working intuitively with others involved in the Plan through their dreams and other unconscious means.

When a child is born there is also a guide that oversees this process, just as there is special guide who oversees the transition into death. These guides remain with individuals only long enough to see them through these transitions. They generally act as spirit guides for others as well, because the time and energy required for guiding transitions is limited. Nonetheless, learning to guide individuals through these transitions is an important learning for each and every being on this level.

Another guide that is usually involved at an early age is one who is familiar with the past life history of the child. This guide controls events and people in the child's life along with the spirit guide until it is time for a guide or guides, who are more specialized and can assist the individual in his life task, to take over. Since the life task is often related to the career of the individual, these more specialized guides will usually not become involved until adulthood; hence the necessity of a childhood guide.

The number of guides present at any one time can vary anywhere from two to several hundred. It is very rare to have more than ten or twenty guides at one time, but in extreme cases, individuals have been known to have as many as two or three hundred guides. Individuals with this many guides have usually taken on a task which has critical effects for many and for the course of history. Most individuals have two or three primary guides, including the spirit guide, who stay with them at all times and a few others who come and go as needed. Even the primary guides, outside of the spirit guide, eventually give way to others as tasks or lessons are completed and they are no longer needed.

As an individual becomes ready to begin the life task, appropriate guides arrive to work along with the spirit guide and any remaining primary guides. If the life task changes or shifts over the course of a lifetime, as it often does, other guides may be needed, and those no longer needed may depart. There are also guides who act as consutants for the primary guides, but who are not involved on a day-to-day basis. There are no special names for the various primary guides that come and go throughout the lifetime; they will be identified according to their specialty. There are healing guides for those involved in healing work, musical guides for musicians, technological guides for technicians, and so forth. But the most significant guide is the spirit guide who understands the particular personality of the individual and is, therefore, better able to predict the individual's behavior. He serves an important function in assisting other guides in working with the individual until they too become accustomed to the individual's personality.

Beyond the astral plane lies another called the causal plane, which in inhabited by beings such as ourselves, called entities. Although the guides of the higher astral plane are able to perform a number of functions at once, entities have the ability to attend simultaneously to many more tasks than these guides. Entities are created by the reunion of around a thousand souls, and as result, are able to perform diverse and complex tasks. In some ways they operate like little cities with instantaneous and perfectly functioning communication systems, because each entity is actually one Mind.

Entities are not only involved in matters pertaining to the earth, but they may also be involved with other planets and other realities. Before becoming an entity, a being must remain in the reincarnational system that he arose from. When one becomes an entity, the ability to be involved in other reincarnational systems evolves, so that work can be carrried out on other planets and in other systems of reality. A being or an entity can become involved in any plane whose vibration is lower than that of their own. Thus entities act as guides to astral beings just as astral beings act as guides to those on the physical plane. There are those beyond the causal plane who are assisting entities in their work and in their growth as well. We are not able to describe planes beyond our realm, just as you are not able to know those beyond yours except via a medium.

Those on the causal plane sometimes work with individuals, but more commonly, they oversee processes on earth and elsewhere. They act as guides to the personal guides. Some of the tasks we perform would not be understandable to you. Our tasks beyond those of acting as guide and teacher for earth are best left unspecified, but we can describe more fully our involvement with earth.

We are not only speaking for ourselves but for many like us who are working with the earth and her people. We have done so for millenniums, and we will continue to do so for many millenniums to come. Just as spirit guides act in ways that facilitate individuals' growth and accomplishment of the tasks they have set for themselves, we act as guides for earth, guiding her destiny and facilitating her evolvement. The earth is a living being, as you are coming to realize, with a purpose and an evolutionary path. The earth is currently undergoing a shift in vibrational level which is partly responsible for some of the current changes in weather and topography. This is all part of her natural evolutionary course. However, it is being interfered with to some extent by humankind's polluting ways, for humans are treating the earth as a garbage dump for their technology.

This is perhaps our greatest concern, for your politics will iron themselves out, but it may take many hundreds of years for the earth to recover from humankind's careless ways. Along these lines much has already been said by others like ourselves. But our task is not so much to guide individuals as to guide the planet. This includes, at times, guiding its leaders; in this sense, we do act as individual guides. There are other individuals whom we seek out to assist us in our work, and we work with them mainly intuitively, although we will speak to those who are able to listen.

Another task which entities perform is to assist in the reunion of the entity mates. This process of reunion is similar to the birth process. Integration and coordination of the various faculties must be learned and a certain amount of growing up must be accomplished before full functioning is available to the entity.

The work that those on our level of existence do through mediums is primarily that of instruction, although personal guidance is often part of this. We do not seek, however, to become overly involved in the comings and goings of each individual human drama, but prefer to assist in providing those in a human body with a broad understanding of their Plan and the purpose of life in general. Thus we do not act as guides to specific problems. If a problem arises that requires specialized guidance— for instance, medical— we call on guides in the higher astral whose main function is providing this type of assistance. Thus each being has a specialized role, and this is also true among the entities. We each have chosen certain areas pertaining to earth upon which to focus our energies; that way we do not duplicate tasks or interfere with the work of other entities. Because we are better able to communicate with each other than you are, coordination is far simpler than it is for those on the material plane.

Life is highly organized; each entity has a purpose, and we serve it to the best of our ability. We grow and evolve in the same manner that you do— through making choices and learning from the results of those choices. This does not change as one advances along the evolutionary path. What does change is one's perceptions, for our view of life is far different from that of the average man or woman. We are in a unique situation of having experienced all that you have experienced or ever will experience in the human body. We have also experienced all the lessons of the astral plane and many on this plane as well. From this perspective we are able to offer understanding about the human condition and its state of evolution, and we will do so when asked. We feel it is very important for this understanding to reach your planet, particularly at a time so crucial to the earth's evolution and well-being.

The messages one receives from our level of reality will be quite different in content than those received from astral beings. Their perception of life does not greatly differ, but their involvement and purpose in communicating is quite different. They will communicate in answer to most questions of a personal nature, whereas we prefer to limit our communication to more global issues; this is the main difference. For the most part, those on the higher astral plane are capable of fine guidance, but a word of caution is in order here in regard to prediction.

The future is not set. We are continually creating our futures by our current choices. Even those aspects of one's Plan that may appear set are actually sketched out only in general, with the specifics waiting to be created by the individual. It is important to understand this when questioning about the future. Future prediction is very difficult for even the most advanced and experienced of us. It is even more difficult for those on the astral than it is on the causal, so care must be taken when receiving information of this nature. One must receive it with the understanding that it may or may not be true and that most circumstances can change from one moment to the next. Misinformation is never given intentionally from our level or from the higher astral, but mistakes can be made even by us because of the nature of life, which progresses on the basis of freedom of choice.

Those beings who choose to offer predictive information do so at the risk of being incorrect. Sometimes the risk in being wrong outweighs the benefits that may be achieved by offering a piece of information. On the other hand, sometimes the benefits are well worth the risks. Each situation is individual, and it is part of the lessons of those beings abiding on the astral and causal planes to exercise judgment in these matters. Those on the causal plane have more experience in exercising their judgment on these matters, so the likelihood of receiving not only information that is correct but information that is ultimately helpful is greatly increased.

We do not advise asking specific questions pertaining to your future. If answers are to be had, knowing them is rarely helpful; so they are best left unexplored. More often than not, the desire to know the specifics of the future comes from the ego's need to control things in order to feel safe. We suggest that all who approach these levels of intelligence do so with a discriminating mind and with the goal of understanding the soul's Plan and life in general rather than that of knowing the specifics of a situation.

There are things that are under one's control and things that are not. We must learn to create our lives in the fashion we desire while accepting the fact that all we desire may not manifest, but that all we need for our growth will. Everything we meet in life serves a purpose. It is for us to try to uncover this purpose in order to make life more meaningful and to facilitate our acceptance of circumstances that are beyond our control. This is not an easy attitude to integrate, and one is usually very far along in one's evolution before this is accomplished. Nevertheless, this attitude is necessary in obtaining a perspective that gives one the understanding needed to move through life gracefully.

The kinds of questions most appropriate to ask are those that do not ask which course to follow, but rather seek to understand the overall Plan so that one can better choose a course of action oneself. Questions about one's daily comings and goings such as, "What should I do with my old car?" "What kind of car should I buy next?" "When will I die?" "Where is the ring I lost?" and so forth are not appropriate. They are not appropriate, because they are short-sighted and seek only to allay the ego's fears and support its needs. The ego is that part of us that is sometimes out of step with that part of ourselves we call the Higher Self, or soul. When we allow the ego's desires and needs to dominate, we may become alienated from life, from others, and from our Higher Selves. These types of questions seek to control life and to make life more comfortable or easier for the ego. That is not the goal of life any more than pain and discomfort are the goal. The goal is to move through life as best we can, learning from our choices and making the best of the experiences our soul presents us. We are here to learn through the choices we make; that is how we grow and evolve.

The choice process is integral to one's spiritual development. When the choice process is tampered with by individuals— in the body or out of the body— one's spiritual development is hampered. That creates some karma for both those who have usurped the free will of the individual and for the individual who has surrendered his free will. Learning not to give one's power away to others— that is, learning to not allow others to make choices for us— is a major lesson of the physical plane experience. For those who have a tendency to give their power away to others, channeling is particularly dangerous, for these individuals assume that non-physical beings are more capable of telling them what to do than they themselves are capable of knowing. In their minds, it is not a matter of making their own choice, but in making the "right choice," which they assume is more likely to come from a non-physical being than from themselves or another individual. In reality, there are no "right" choices—only choices. We are here to learn from *our* choices, not from the choices others make for us, although that is a lesson in itself.

Questions such as, "How can I best deal with this situation?" "What is the meaning of this experience for me?" "How can I best understand this event in the context of my life?" are all good. They are asking for more information upon which choices can be based. This is vastly different than asking which choice to make. Knowing which questions are appropriate and which are not is an important aspect of handling the channeling experience in a positive manner. More will be said about this in a later chapter.

The kinds of beings one will encounter on each plane of existence will vary in terms of their interests, their needs, and to some extent their personalities. Personality is something that falls away as one moves through the astral plane and beyond. Evidence of personality is also evidence of one's level of evolvement, or lack thereof. Beings who express distinct personality characteristics, dialects, and other vestiges of former earthly existences may be entertaining and well meaning, but their information may lack veracity. One should be guarded about accepting information, particularly personal information offered by those astral beings whose personalities remain intact. These beings have not developed to the level of being able to read the ethers to the extent that others beyond the personality level have. This is perhaps the most reliable means for evaluating the level of the being to whom you may be speaking. Entities, for the most part are very straightforward and formal in their speech, and they do not cajole or seek your approval through charm or sense of humor. A sense of humor is something present at all levels, but how one uses it is critical to this discussion. Any attempt on the part of a being to win your favor through clever antics, humor, charm, or personal mannerisms is to be suspect. There is no need for those with a worthy message to win the attention of humans. We are not attached to your responses nor will we change our ways in order to please you. We offer our information honestly and with respect for your freedom to believe or not to believe it.

Be on guard for those who offer unsolicited information. The motive is crucial here. Some of the possible motives may be to please you, to encourage you to channel, or to try to win your trust. The only acceptable motive for offering information is to facilitate the soul's Plan; yet, even this information, if unsolicited by you may unduly interrupt the course you are freely choosing. This is an important principle in our realm: People must first ask for information. Those on the higher astral plane do not often make this mistake nor do they offer information in order to win someone's attention. For the most part, only those still on the reincarnational path, seeking human companionship and distraction from the task at hand are apt to do this. Let us say a little more about these individuals and their style.

Personality and dialect are particularly apparent in speaking to these individuals and reveal their lack of development. They need to be encouraged to return to their tasks on the lower astral so that they can continue their learning. Many of them are upset and frightened about their current condition and seek solace among human beings. Many are seeking simple companionship and are relatively harmless and not very persistent in their pursuance of this. There are those, however, who are deeply troubled, who miss the pleasures of the flesh, and who will do anything in their power to get what they believe they need. These individuals can be very clever and persistent, devising elaborate plots and schemes to entrap unsuspecting ouija board players or developing mediums. They will say anything to keep the communication going, and many will imitate guides to convince naive human beings of the truth of what they have to say. Once they are found out, they will usually leave, but some simply take on a new persona and continue the old game. Indulging in conversation with these types is a waste of time, not only for you but for them.

These disturbed individuals must be told in no uncertain terms that you are unwilling to speak with them and that they must go and attend to their lessons. It is important to explain to them the damage they are doing to others and to themselves in carrying on this activity. They do not have a realistic idea of the impact they have on those on earth; it is just a game to them. To them, it is fun to see people disappointed when something they have said turns out to be false. It may be difficult for you to understand how they can be so insensitive, but this problem exists because they are both undeveloped and out of the body. In a sense, they are like children, and they must be taught that what they are doing is harmful. Fearing them only feeds their involvement with you, because it adds to their fun. These individuals cannot hurt you, for they are only capable of speaking to you, and you have total control over this. Nevertheless, many humans are deeply frightened by their antics. This fear draws to them others of equal development, making these planes appear to be populated only by these types, which is not the case.

These beings need the kind of compassion and firmness you would give a naughty child. Stop all communication with them so they will lose interest and leave; otherwise you run the risk of having them continue speaking to you in another guise. People who are just developing their channeling abilities will have contacts with this level of reality and may not be able to reach higher levels. If this is the case, it is best to wait before exploring this ability any further, for nothing good can come of speaking to those that reside on the lower astral. The ins and outs of development will be addressed shortly in another chapter. The point to be made now is that you must be very discriminating about whom you talk with, and you must approach channeling with the proper attitude.

The proper approach to these and higher levels of reality is to rely on inner guidance above all else and keep outside guidance in its proper place. No one can tell you anything that you cannot discover within your own being. A corollary to this is that much of what others tell you may not fit for you. A continual sifting process must occur when taking in information from any source, which involves continual evaluation of every aspect of the information based intuitively on how it fits you. Each piece of information must be checked out intuitively before it is accepted as true. However, not everyone's intuition and ability to discriminate are developed enough to make them reliable. Individuals for whom this is true are especially vulnerable to misinformation obtained from channeling, and this makes dabbling in channeling and channeled material particularly dangerous for them. It is best for these individuals to discover what is right for them on their own through trial and error or to seek information and advise from only the most reputable sources. They should not attempt to channel or become involved with amateur channels.

These realms should also be approached with the understanding that just as no one in the body is infallible, no one out of it is either. Even those on the highest planes make misjudgments and mistakes. You will not find any of us on the higher astral and above who claim infallibility, yet many who approach us believe we are. This belief is one of the greatest roadblocks to healthy communication with us. It leads to giving up one's power to choose, and that is the ultimate crime against life.

Another problematic assumption people have is that we are able to know everything. We have access to information that you do not, but that does not mean we have access to *all* information. This is an important point, because in addition to not being infallible, we are also not omnipresent or omnipotent. We can monitor more than one activity at a time, but we cannot monitor every activity on the planet at once. There are limits to our intelligence, just as there are limits to yours; our limits are simply beyond yours. As consciousness evolves, so do one's capabilities; but we are still in the process of evolving our consciousness and have our limitations as well.

Another difficulty that may lead to misunderstanding about our capabilities lies in the differences in our conceptions of time and space. These varying perceptions are sometimes at the root of miscalculations. People often expect us to be familiar with your geography, your concept of history, and your sense of time. But those acting as guides must reorientate themselves in order to be able to speak in the time and space terms you are familiar with. Our conception of a mile, for instance, may not match yours. When mistakes are made in these kinds of calculations, people often jump to the conclusion that everything we said was false. The differences between your reality and ours must be understood in order to avoid blanket rejections of this sort.

This brings us to another important point: Because we make a mistake on occasion, does not invalidate all information we have to offer. We admittedly are not perfect, but much of what we have to offer is valuable and offered with care and wisdom. We hope to increase your ability to relate to us in a healthy manner by admitting our imperfections without having these imperfections be reason for totally disregarding what we have to say. It is, of course, up to you to accept or reject what we have to offer; but total acceptance and total rejection are simply two sides of the same coin of non-discrimination.

Education about these realms beyond the senses and about the capabilities and limitations of those who inhabit these realms is necessary before people are able to make proper use of information coming from them. When it is understood that the sources may be of varying levels of ability, it becomes clear why so much of what is known as channeled material is inconsistent and untrustworthy.

First of all, those who reside on the lower astral plane, those awaiting reincarnation, have certain abilities that are paranormal from your way of thinking, but their abilities in no way make them fit to act as advisors, guides, or prognosticators, although some of them want you to believe they can do these things. Their way of seeing differs from your way of seeing, however. They no longer have physical eyes, of course, so they have no specific sensory mechanism. Instead, they are able to sense energy fields via their own energy field. This sensing process is similar to feeling, but it is not tactile in any way. This is an instance where words fail because their experience is not like any experience known to you.

Nevertheless, in their own way, they are aware of people's thoughts, feelings, and desires. The astral plane is the plane of desire where one's desires, feelings, and thoughts manifest in an almost physical way. Thought forms, similar to pictures, are constantly being created on the astral plane by humans, and they can be read by even those only temporarily out of the body. Because the stronger one's thoughts or desires are, the stronger the thought form will be, those reading these thought forms know what is most important to someone and what they are creating for themselves. Lower astral beings make predictions by reading back to humans what they are creating, which is often what psychics do as well. What they are unable to know, however, is the individual's Plan and how it is intertwined with these creations. Thus because their predictions are based on incomplete information, they have limited value. This is not to say that there will be not truth in what they say— and this is what can be so tricky— but what they say will be only partly true, making it all the more misleading.

When speaking to lower astral beings, you will not only obtain insufficient or inaccurate information but information that may be detrimental to your growth, because they lack the ability to determine what is or is not helpful to you. Anyway, their motivation is rarely to assist you but to meet their own needs; and in most cases, they will try to do this any way they can.

Lower astral beings are not able to read past lives, but they can tell what someone believes to be in his past and what others have told him about it, which they often use to sound authoritative. Offering past life information and pretending to know something about a loved one who has passed on are two of their favorite ways of building an alliance. They also enjoy making up information about death, lost articles, stock market tips, soul mates, and what will happen in the future, but only because these are the favorite topics of those seeking to communicate with these realms.

Lower astral beings are very wise to the ways that people are most vulnerable. In fact, they band together with others who are involved in similar endeavors and share pointers and former experiences. In this way, they become very clever about how to deal with human beings in ways that will be satisfying to them. They are con artists, and the same scams are used over and over again. One reason they get away with these things is the lack of information available to people about these realms. In addition, people who have been conned are usually too ashamed to discuss this with others, and that allows the scams to continue. Just as your consumer advocates are working to divest certain con artists of their power through education of the public, others like ourselves seek to educate those who are interested in these realms in hopes of divesting these individuals of their games and forcing them back to their appointed lessons. Their game-playing is a problem, and delivering the necessary information to people involved in these realms is a way of correcting this problem.

In the interest of education, let us look at a few of the favorite scams of some residents of the lower astral plane. The first and most common scenario involves claiming that they are the questioner's guide and that they have been trying to contact him or her. This flatters the individual, making him feel important, and justifies use of the ouija board. Usually at this point they will tell the individual something very special he wants to hear about himself— flattery gets them everywhere. Favorite lines are that he will become famous, wealthy, meet the person of his dreams, and so forth. The being simply reads the desires of the person he is speaking to and tells him these desires will be realized. At this point, the individual is usually quite curious and anxious to continue, though even he may doubt what he hears. Nonetheless, the hook has been taken, and a relationship is in the making.

The next step is for the being to win the individual's trust. This is usually done by telling him something about himself that may not be easily known to an ordinary stranger. People who fall for this don't understand that it is simple for these beings to obtain basic life information about the living, especially when they have opened themselves up to astral beings by talking with them. The beings either obtain it through reading their thoughts or the thoughts of others in the room, or by investigating other thought forms on the astral plane. Beings of this caliber often seek the information they need to build trust even before responding to unsuspecting individuals who are playing with the ouija board, the most common method of contact for non-mediums.

For individuals who are not mediums and do not have the development to contact higher intelligences, these boards are particularly dangerous. They allow those who cannot contact any but the lowest levels of the astral to do so, with no hope of contacting a higher energy who could lead them away from the ploys of those on the lower astral. It is another story for mediums who contact these realms with a ouija board; there is hope for them. The fact that some are able to use the ouija board successfully is, unfortunately, an encouragement to many who do not understand that a certain level of development is necessary to gain access to guides and teachers who have more to offer than tricks and fantasies.

Another way lower astral beings build trust at this stage is to talk in glowing terms about Love , Peace, Light, and God. It is remarkable how well some of these beings are able to imitate beings who have tried to teach them of these things. They are like children mocking their teachers through skillful imitation, but they have not learned their lessons, only the right words and how to say them. This is usually enough for many people to be convinced that they have a friend on the other side who may not be trustworthy in terms of information, but who is certainly not the demon one must watch out for on these planes. The fact that most people have a conception of either Devils or angels residing on these planes stands in the way of proper discrimination, because they conclude that a being will sound good if he is good and sound bad if he is bad. This belief, if properly examined, would fail the test of logical analysis, but many people set logic and analysis aside when relating to these realms, being lost in the exotic lure and the promise of knowing things one has not been able to know before.

At this point, the person is usually trying to sort out the good information from the bad, while coming up with more questions. It is also at about this time that others may be brought into the intrigue, increasing the potential for damage to the individual's life. An enmeshed relationship is established which is likely to continue until the individual confronts the being after discovering that a majority of the information given was false. But each time beings are confronted they have a reason or excuse for the mistake made, which throws their trustworthiness into question once again. Because people want to believe that they have access to answers to their questions, they are often willing to put up with wrong answers and excuses. Sometimes, individuals carry this out so long and believe so diligently in what they have been told that it affects their friends, their work, their marriages, their daily functioning, and every current decision. People have been known to leave relationships, move, quit jobs, start relationships, get pregnant, and make other major decisions based on advise or information received from these realms. You must always be aware of why you are making a decision. Beware of making any decision based on channeled information alone. Some people are more prone to giving their power away than others. Those who are prone to this are better off leaving channeling and channeled material alone until they have become more clear about their own needs and desires.

Desperate beings such as this will hold onto a relationship with the living as long as they can, and they will try anything to keep people involved. Befriending the people they are talking with is a common tactic. They chat with them, listen to their problems, flatter them, and tell them what they want to hear. Another tactic is to offer to teach them about something. These beings are able to read the knowledge you hold in your own mind and read it back to you, which results in their sounding very educated about subjects you are familiar with. All the books you have ever read, all of your experiences, and all of your thoughts are stored in the unconscious and can be read from the astral plane. Thus even these lower astral beings are able to describe details from your childhood, read passages from books, and anticipate your areas of interest. Some are more skillful than others at reading from one's Book of Knowledge, but even the most amateur is capable of doing this to some extent. In the same way, they are able to know things about family, relatives, and friends with whom you are emotionally connected. They simply follow the energy cords that connect you to others and read their Books. Once you open yourself up to these beings by speaking with them, you, in a sense, give them permission to read your energy and the energies of those connected to you.

The way they keep the relationship going is by being whatever they feel you want the most. If you want a friend, they will be that; if you want a teacher, they will be that; and if you want a lover, they will be happy to oblige with that as well. Without getting into this subject in any detail, suffice to say, that many on the astral are looking for vicarious thrills, and some will seek to form lover-like relationships in order to satisfy their longing for closeness and yours at the same time, if you happen to have this need. There are ways they can present suggestions about this to people that make this kind of relationship seem perfectly acceptable and advantageous. They use the information they have about you to mold and manipulate you to meet their needs, usually under the guise of doing something for you. They appear selfless and disinterested in their own needs and only interested in yours, when the reality is quite the opposite.

In summary, the course of the first scam is basically this: These desperate beings establish trust by telling their victims what they already know about themselves and what they want to hear. This paves the way for acceptance of false information about past lives and the future, which their victims have no way of verifying, but which they will accept because trust has been built and because they misunderstand the capabilities of the beings with whom they are communicating. This sets the stage for one disappointment after another as they discover the trusted information about the future is not accurate or reliable. Nevertheless, this may not be enough for some to discontinue the relationship; instead, it only places it on a more confrontational ground, one that challenges the being to prove his knowledge. If the relationship is flagging and the being senses that he may lose it anyway, he may retaliate be trying to induce fear or by belittling the victim. If the relationship cannot be saved, he at least gets a charge out of the fear, hurt, anger, and shame he has managed to produce. Most people in this situation are utterly shocked that anyone—especially someone with whom they had a trusted relationship—could be so cruel and deceitful. Let it be understood that those who act in this manner are very young souls who are desperately unhappy with their current lot in life (in death!).

A second common scenario is very different from the last. In this one, the being takes on a role of "poor me, I am so alone and in need of a friend." There is usually some truth to this, but it is a ploy nonetheless. They attempt to befriend the living by appearing very harmless, helpless, and pitiful. They observe those playing with ouija boards and select individuals with whom they feel these tactics will work— those who are kindhearted, savior types. They usually have a very sad story to tell regarding their terrible plight on the astral plane and how no one understands their needs. They usually have a strong attachment to earth, as do most who play these games, and for some reason or another refuse to accept their non-physical condition. Addictions of any kind, a traumatic death, or compulsive attachments to certain individuals may explain their lack of acceptance, but often it is simply a case of being afraid of the new place they have moved to and their own unwillingness to accept the love and guidance offered to them.

These beings will ask whomever they are speaking to to do things for them: to contact relatives, to give messages to others, or to complete a task they left undone. These may or may not be real requests; some beings are merely copying this scenario from others who have been sincere about these requests. Some beings just enjoy getting people to follow their directions and finding new ways to gain control of physical plane matters by manipulating people. To these individuals, it is all a game, but some are truly distressed and seeking help in the only way they know how— through people on the material plane instead of through those who are truly capable of helping them on the astral plane.

The third scenario is usually short-lived but impactful, and an impact is exactly what the beings engaging in this scheme are seeking. Their scheme is to frighten, shock, appall, and anger whomever is unfortunate enough to speak with them. They become the Devil personified. Because of the religious beliefs of many, a majority of people are very easily frightened be these tactics. True fear and disgust are inspired by these beings, and they enjoy it immensely. They find it humorous and exciting to have this kind of power over individuals. If they find that you do not react in fear but laugh at them and send them on their way, they are likely to leave you alone. But, just as the others seek those who are apt to fall for their ploys, these beings seek those who are most easily frightened. These are the games that have had a great deal of impact on the reinforcement of the concepts of the Devil, demons, possession, and so forth.

Your conception of these planes has been shaped by your Judeo-Christian beliefs in heaven and hell, God and the Devil, and Original Sin. The concept of Original Sin is at the root of your belief in the dichotomy of life: Man is separate from God and therefore evil by nature. This kind of dichotomizing has given rise to fear of that which is different. There is a human tendency to see oneself and all who are like oneself as good, and to see those who are unlike oneself as bad. This has been the rationale for many a war and much hatred all in the name of your so-called God or good. The understanding has not yet come to light of the goodness of all life and the rightness inherent in every decision, even the most heinous, for all choices lead to learning and growth, and that is the purpose. The entire philosophical and religious foundation of your culture needs to be upturned to include new perspectives on life that no longer dichotomize and divide.

We all live the same life, but we are each unique expressions of this one life. We have been given the freedom to make our own choices so that we can develop our uniqueness and learn the lessons of the physical plane. That which is known as evil to you is better understood to be or a choice that brings greater difficulty, and that which is known as good to you is a choice that brings greater love. That which is known as evil also leads to greater love but via a more circuitous route than that of a wiser choice. Perhaps it is best to categorize good and evil as wise and unwise choices, for although some choices bring greater pain than others, all choices lead to love, for that is all there is.

You carry your concepts of good and evil over to our realm as well, and you assume that those you encounter here will be one or the other. You also assume that you will be able to discern which is which. But because these realms are beyond your senses and do not operate within your sense limitations, your senses are not accurate tools for evaluating them. You need more information about these realms, but you also need a highly developed intuition to discriminate between the false and the true on these planes. If you do not have this tool, you rely on your senses and on logical analysis of the situation, which without proper information about these realms, do not serve you very well.

Throughout history, there have been those capable of contacting these realms through one means or another. This capability, coupled with a lack of knowledge and a lack of intuitive development, has led to the creation of an entire body of knowledge about these realms which we would categorize as primarily distorted. Your exploration of these realms is analogous to a blind man studying an oil painting and declaring it to be a series of bumps. Thus uninformed and unskilled explorations into these realms have led to conclusions that conjure up images of demons, capable of possession and the most heinous deeds, and angels with golden harps and halos. The demons are apparently the lower astral beings, who present themselves as frightful in some cases, and the angels are your interpretation of those such as ourselves who offer comfort.

More will be said later on the subject of possession, but let it be known that possession as you think of it is so rare an occurrence that, for all practical purposes it is non-existent. Someone who is not a medium cannot be possessed, and no one can be possessed against his will. The lower astral beings are no more able to possess you than they are able to carry out other deeds on the physical plane. They are only able to affect matter under certain circumstances, and only by using the energy of living individuals. Just as the energy of mediums can be used to transport trumpets and other objects, so the energy of others can be used to produce poltergeist phenomena. The most these lost souls are able to do is bang doors, rock rocking chairs, creak floor boards, and so on. They are not able to pick you up, move you, or physically affect you in any way, although some try to do this by frightening you in hopes that your fear will bring the results they desire (such as leaving the "haunted" home).

The astral souls who haunt homes are stuck between life and death. They cannot go back to the life they were living, and they refuse to go on to the life they must live. These lost souls must be told to accept their death and go with their guides. There are a number of recommended standard phrases to use in speaking with them: "I command you to return from whence you came. Be gone in the name of love" is the most common. Often, you can help them before sending them away by speaking with them about the folly of communicating with humans and of trying to return to the earth plane. You must explain to them that their communication is hurtful to you and to themselves and that they must attend to their lessons and listen to their guides, who are waiting to show them what they need to do. Sometimes these souls will listen to the living who say this to them, when they will not listen to those of us on this side. It is important to speak to them firmly and caringly without fear. If they think you are vulnerable to their ploys or insincerities, they will try to continue with you or go on to the next individual.

The capabilities of those on the lower astral plane have been grossly overestimated by the living. They cannot cause physical harm, because they have no physical means with which to carry this out. They cannot affect physical matter in any appreciable way nor can they speak to you if you do not want them to. The only means by which they can affect you is through your fear and your willingness to continue to speak to them and believe what they say. Words cannot hurt you if you do not give them the power to do so. Likewise, the fear they try to instill in you cannot take hold if you are educated and do not fall prey to their false ploys. You truly have all the power in these realms, and they have none. If they had the power to do some of the things they pretend to be able to do, they would probably not be so unhappy. The source of their unhappiness is their inability to affect matter as they previously could. They envy those in the body and attempt to scare and seduce them to regain some semblance of what they knew in the past. It is a sad situation, indeed, and these individuals need your compassion and your firmness— not your fear or sympathy.

It is also important to understand the capabilities of those on the higher astral plane and those like ourselves on the causal plane, so that you have appropriate expectations of what we can and cannot do. People are also far more likely to ask appropriate questions if they understand the capabilities and limitations of the source.

It should be obvious by now that the state of being of those who are no longer part of the reincarnational system is vastly different from those who remain in this system. Those who have gone beyond reincarnation have gained wisdom from their experiences, and although they have their own lessons, will be equipped to act as teachers and guides for those remaining within this system once they have been prepared. The preparation takes place on the mid-astral plane where instruction is given in maneuvering on the astral and in guiding others. Those who are training to be guides will act in an apprentice role with others who are more experienced until they reach a level of understanding that enables them to act independently, at which time they are said to reside on the higher astral level. Those on the earth plane do not, for the most part, come in contact with these guides-in-training, because these beings are not allowed to speak directly through mediums or to act independently. They act only in concert with others like themselves under the tutelage of guides. The situation is a little like your schools where individuals are not treated individually but en masse.

Those on the higher astral have graduated to guiding at least one individual at a time. As their proficiency increases, they adopt more. A guide's capabilities extend to as many as three or four full-time individuals and a few others with whom they spend occasional periods. Their duties involve studying the past life history, current lessons and tasks, and future lives of those they are guiding. Time is not linear in our realm but concurrent, so past and future lives are as much of a reality as present ones. However, it takes greater skill to read the past and future than it does to read the present. One of the most difficult aspects of their work as guides is learning to read these things accurately.

Another difficult aspect of a guide's task is learning to anticipate the moves of the individual so that they can better facilitate the soul's Plan. The individual is constantly making choices that create his future, and these creations are interwoven with the soul's lessons by the guide who acts as a tool for the Higher Self of the individual. Guides speak intuitively to the individual and to others involved in his Plan in order to affect the required lessons. The guides and others like ourselves are able to make an impact on events only in this way, for we cannot affect matter any more than lower astral beings. However, the power to affect individuals intuitively should not be underestimated.

Another task of the guide is to monitor the dream life of the individual and to insert messages into the dreams that are in keeping with the soul's Plan. This is the primary means of communication with the Higher Self for those who are unable to receive messages in other ways.

For those who are channels or mediums, guides also provide a kind of protection that prohibits other beings from communicating with them without the channel's permission. This service is provided only to those who have earned it, though. One must first learn the ins and outs of this realm through exposure to it without protection. In this way, discrimination and other necessary lessons are taught.

Through continual contact with the one who is being guided, the guide is able to anticipate how he will react to events in his life and what choices he will make. This insight is helpful for any other guides or teachers who are working with him but do not have continual or lengthy contact. The spirit guide is able to coach others in what they can expect and how best to accomplish their appointed tasks. This guidance process is not as much like puppetry as it might sound. In reality, we are not as separate from you as it seems. We are all one Being, and it is rather more like the hands of the body opening doors for the rest of the body to walk through. It is not manipulation, for there are no ulterior motives, only those of the Higher Self. Guides work only for the good of all and do nothing to interfere with the free will of the individual, which is greatly respected by them.

It is the knowledge gained about the individual through continual contact that allows the guide to do his work as well as he does (there is no gender on these planes, but a pronoun is required here). Because it is not easy for others who are not constantly with an individual to read someone, in a channeling session for instance, they usually confer with his spirit guide to obtain information rather than delving into the ethers themselves. It is not always clear that it takes time and energy to understand someone; it is assumed that beings other than the spirit guide also have instantaneous knowledge of the person to whom they are speaking, and this simply is not true. Other beings do, however, have easy access to the spirit guide, and given sufficient time to communicate with him, they are able to respond to questions by combining information obtained from the guide with their own immediate sense of the person. In most cases, causal entities are able to deliver more information, because they are able to read the past lives and future a little more reliably than most on the higher astral planes. Most readings performed by mediums, however, involve higher astral guides and not causal entities.

The task of reading one's past lives is complicated by the fact that there is no clear way of knowing the exact circumstances of those lives. Thus if you are told you were a merchant in the fifteenth century, the specific details of this existence— the daily experiences— are not available. What is available are the events, people, and circumstances that had a profound effect on your course and the progress of your Plan. This fact is not widely understood, but helps to clarify some of the confusion and disappointment some feel when they receive a reading. However, even if these details were available, there would be no reason for delivering this kind of information. In fact, much information that is available is never delivered, because it would serve no purpose, and the course chosen by the individual might be affected. Information is carefully dispensed with the understanding that it might change the choices the individual will make in the future. It is never dispensed in a way that suggests what specific choice to make, although *general* suggestions may be made to place the person, hopefully, more firmly on course. Thus every detail of the past and future is not available to those reading the individual, although the spirit guide and other primary guides will know the specifics of the current life.

Another limitation lies in our ability to communicate with others, even through a channel or medium. At times, it is difficult to translate our concepts into so limited a form of language. Some of us are also hindered by our lack of skill with a certain language. It takes a great deal of study to master a language and its colloquialisms. Furthermore, it is necessary for us to be aware of the current cultural trends, customs, and fads, in order to adequately understand and address questions put to us. If we do not understand the context from which the questions arise— both the cultural and individual—we run the risk of being misunderstood. We do our best to be understood, but there are times when others misconstrue even the clearest of statements. We have no control over this.

This last point is another limitation of the work we do, for it is not possible to correct or restate what we have said when it appears that others are misusing the information they received. Thus information is given, and individuals will do what they will with it. Some hang onto every word as if it came from God. They read and reread the transcript of our conversation as if doing so will somehow give them the answers they are looking for. Too often they are looking for someone to tell them what will happen in the future so that they can feel in control. Other times, they find solace in the words and look to them for support in times of despair, which is a positive use of the dialogue and one of our purposes in speaking to people. People often become stuck in despair and hope-lessness, unable to see their part in the Greater Scheme or the part their lessons play in their growth. We try to bring them this under-standing so they can face life with courage and strength of purpose. One should never leave a reading feeling fearful or challenged, but uplifted and enlightened.

We would be remiss if we did not include the limitations of the medium and the channeling process, for we are completely depen-dent upon the skills of the medium for getting our message across. Some distortion—even mistakes—occur from time to time that go uncorrected. For the most part, these distortions and mistakes are minor, and those that are not are corrected. Nevertheless, there is an element of unpredictability in this, and we must do our best to adjust to these mistakes. When a mistake is made, correcting it can sometimes lead to distrust on the part of the one receiving the message, so it is important for all to understand that this happens and that it is not a reason to distrust the entire message.

We have attempted to introduce you to the basics of channeling in this first chapter. The following chapters will hopefully answer your remaining questions by giving you detailed information about what we have merely touched upon in this one.

CHAPTER II

WHO CAN CHANNEL?

Who can and cannot channel and why, the questions most in need of answering, deserve a detailed explanation including some understanding of evolution. Some people can channel and some cannot; and many of those who can, are unable to do it reliably. This last point is key. The development of a channel requires lifetimes of preparation; the mere presence of this ability does not insure its reliability. Further explanation requires an understanding of the evolutionary process.

Evolution proceeds in stages or cycles sometimes known as the Infant, Baby, Young, Mature, and Old cycles. When a soul first enters the earth's reincarnational system, he or she does so as an Infant soul. After many hundreds of years and many lifetimes in one cycle, the individual progresses to the next. Each cycle has its lessons, which must be mastered before a soul can move on to the next cycle. Each cycle builds upon the last, and all previous learning is retained.

Each of the levels— Infant, Baby, Young, Mature, and Old— has within it seven levels. The first level of each cycle resembles the former cycle, and the last level in each cycle resembles the next cycle. The first and last levels are, therefore, transition levels. The remaining levels— second, third, fourth, fifth, and sixth— are those in which the majority of the lessons of that level are met and accomplished. Because the sixth level is usually considered the most difficult of the levels, many souls spend more lifetimes in the sixth level of each cycle than in the other levels.

The ability to channel usually begins to develop at around the second or third level of the Old cycle if the individual chooses to acknowledge it. If it goes unacknowledged, it may develop very slowly and never fully develop over the entire course of one's reincarnations. Not everyone fully develops this or any other psychic ability before leaving the reincarnational system; full development of these abilities is not a prerequisite to moving beyond the physical plane. Some experience with these abilities, however, is required, mostly as a means for accomplishing certain lessons involved in the development of these abilities. The lessons are related to correct use of power, discrimination, and trusting oneself. Some individuals choose to focus their energies on developing this or other psychic skills and may become fully developed in the late fifth or sixth levels of the Old cycle. Thus you cannot be sure whether or not you are sufficiently developed by knowing your level, but knowing this can indicate that possibility. You can obtain this information by asking someone on the higher astral or above who is familiar with you. Be sure to have a reliable channel obtain this information for you, because you may not be able to trust information received by yourself. Those below the fifth level of the Old cycle are not likely to be encouraged to channel or to view their channeling as reliable.

The question, then, is: How can this ability develop if you don't use it? The answer lies in how you use it, not in never using it. We are suggesting that anyone who is not developed to the fifth level of the Old cycle be very cautious about using this ability and view it with some suspicion. We also feel it would be irresponsible to channel information for others before late level five. The earlier stages of channeling are opportunities to experiment with it in a personal way by evaluating what is received with the intuition and the intellect. It is a time for practicing discrimination, developing your intuition, and learning to trust yourself. Channeling only creates problems if you proceed with total trust in the source and an invested ego rather than humility and discrimination. The wrong attitude will bring painful lessons to those who channel before they are ready.

The fact is that in the early stages of the development of this ability—usually the second, third, and fourth levels of the Old cycle—information received will be inconsistent and unreliable. At times, one may be able to reach one's guide or other higher astral beings; but as often as not, one may only reach into the lower astral beings who are adept at imitating those beyond them. Furthermore, in these early stages of development one has not gained the protection of one's guides, precisely because the lessons of discrimination, correct use of power, and trusting oneself must be learned first. At a certain point in one's development, one gains protection, and the inconsistency ceases. The road to development can be quite rocky if you do not handle the lessons of this phase well.

The lessons of the Old cycle are, in many ways, quite different from those that have gone before. In the earlier cycles, the majority of practical lessons have been learned and talents have been developed. What remains for the Old cycle is a refinement of former lessons and new ones pertaining to experiencing levels of oneself that exist beyond the ego. Prior to the Old cycle, the ego, the personality, the emotions, and the intellect were the focus of growth. In the Old cycle, the spirit becomes the topic of discovery, as one loosens one's attachment to the personal identity and the glamor-izing of the ego and begins to yearn for the realms beyond the senses, beyond the material. Many old souls seek solace in religious orders or practices, meditation, retreat from the world, nature, creative expression, and sometimes drugs to meet their need for transcendence of the ego and its gnawing desires. This is a cycle of turning within and experiencing one's spirit to an increasing degree. Along with this change in focus, comes greater sensitivity to the subtle energies to the emotions, the intuition, and the energies that operate beyond the senses.

One of the greatest pitfalls of the Old cycle is in the lure of these unseen realms. Some use spiritual practices as an escape from the dreariness or unhappiness of material existence rather than facing their tasks and lessons in the real world. Unfortunately, rather than making problems go away, avoidance usually magnifies them until the individual is no longer able to ignore them. Bringing one's spirit to the world rather than running from the world is a major lesson of these lifetimes.

Another major pitfall of the early Old cycle is the tendency to be awed by things beyond the senses. This attitude makes naive beginning channels vulnerable to those in the unseen realms if they believe they are contacting a high level of intelligence when they are not. It is also dangerous to assume that all beings who speak through mediums are reliable sources of information and guidance; some are and some are not. You must always evaluate the information you receive with your own intuition— no matter what the source. After all, you are the one who will meet the results of any choices you make based on it.

In the early Old cycle, people who begin to channel will usually do so either with a ouija board or while in meditation. While in meditation, they will either receive short, disjointed phrases or intuitive ideas that they encase in their own words. These intuitive ideas encased in words are actually more trustworthy than the first words you channel, because they come from your intuition and not from outside yourself. The first channeled words are likely to come from your guide, but they may quickly be supplanted by those from beings on the lower astral who see an opportunity for communication. If this occurs, the guide steps aside and allows the others to communicate, for it is part of the developing channel's learning to experience this. From time to time, the guide may intervene and offer support and guidance, but as long as the others continue to interrupt, the guide will allow this to happen. Consequently, the first channeled words are usually a mix of communications from guides and from lower astral beings posing as guides.

If someone's first experiences with channeling occur while using a ouija board, they are more likely than not to communicate with lower astral beings than with any guides. The reason for this is that the presence of a ouija board is a signal to those on the lower astral plane that someone wants to talk, and those willing to oblige come rushing forward, leaving no room for the person's guide, who will not usually assert his presence among the rest. Thus if lower astral beings are present at a ouija board session with an underdeveloped channel they will be given first opportunity to speak; if they are not, the individual may be able to contact his guide, at least until others arrive.

Another factor contributing to difficulties during the early stages of development is the lack of intuitive development. The ability to discriminate develops as the intuition develops, which does not become fully developed for most until around the fifth or sixth levels of the Old cycle. Until discrimination is developed, it is difficult to sense the veracity of the information and its source. This is another reason for discouraging individuals from using their channeling ability until this point. Protection will not be given until the individual is able to discriminate between information given from a lower being and a higher one, and until the person is able to know intuitively what is in his own highest good.

Another major lesson that needs to be learned in the early levels of the Old cycle before protection is given is that of correct use of power. This means not investing your power in others (i.e. allowing discarnate beings to make decisions for you) and not misusing the power that others invest in you. Mediums can fall prey to both types of abuse. Because of the power this ability gives her, a medium is vulnerable to becoming attached to the message she conveys and losing her objectivity. If this happens, she falls prey to being manipulated and delivering misinformation and ineffective guidance. The channel must be just that—a channel for the message—neither interfering with it nor attached to it. It is very important that the medium teach those who come to her how to handle channeled information properly. An entire chapter will be dedicated to this subject, but it is imperative for the medium to remain centered in herself and in her own intuition. If she is ego-involved with her role as a medium, she will be unable to do this.

People give their power away to others, because they believe that someone else has the answers they lack. Let us make it very clear that, first of all, there are no answers. We do not give answers but insight, information, and general guidance. "Answers" implies that there is one correct choice in a matter, and there is not. Every choice leads to learning, as we have said before, and each individual must make his own choices. The choice you make is the correct "answer" for you; the choices others make for you are not. The medium must be very clear in understanding this principle, for if she is not, she runs the risk of abusing her power by suggesting specific answers or applications of the information given. "Abuse of power" means using the power others give you in a way that is harmful to them. Usurping an individual's choice by making the choice is always harmful. Making choices for another, even when they ask you to do so, is an abuse of power, which incurs some degree of karma. Karma is incurred both by the one who invests another with power at the expense of his own growth and by those who accept that power. People in the healing professions in particular have a responsibility to others to keep this from happening.

It is difficult not to feel special when you have an unique ability such as channeling. The antidote to feeling special is recognizing that this ability has been developed by you in previous lives and that it exists solely for the purpose of service. This ability is not to be flaunted but used to serve others. Everyone has certain talents and everyone has a life task which involves these talents. No talent is more valuable than another, just as no life task has more value than another. From the soul's perspective, the ability to channel is a tool for learning lessons and for serving others, as is any other ability. Some of the glamour of channeling comes from the fact that so few people are able to do it. The fact that it seems so mysterious makes it special to some, although just as many are appalled at the thought of it. This brings us to another important point.

Channeling is an area that is fraught with misunderstanding, prejudices, and conflicting viewpoints. Although a channel may receive respect and admiration, he is just as likely to receive disdain, acrimony, and even hatred. If a channel comes to think of himself as special or ordained with a particularly important mission, others will be happy to remind him that they think he is foolish and unstable, if not downright evil. Those who do this work must neither be touched by the praise nor the acrimony if they are to carry it out with integrity. The channel must simply do what he has come here to do to the best of his ability—with humility.

Many people who are involved in the so-called New Age movement are old souls. Only a small percentage of old souls, however, are of the fifth level and above. Many of the early level old souls are not just interested in spirituality and new healing techniques, but are attempting to be the spiritual teachers and healers they are not as yet prepared to be. You might ask: How are you to become qualified if you do not begin somewhere? This is a legitimate question in most professions. However, the work of a spiritual teacher, psychic, or healer takes lifetimes of preparation—not just years.

People in these fields must find more reliable means for determining their readiness.

What is to prevent people from becoming self-proclaimed experts? Nothing currently. There is a need to provide proper training and screening to those who want to do the work of spiritual counseling and healing in its many forms. This is the first step that must be taken in legitimatizing the New Age movement and the techniques it boasts.

How do you determine if you are ready to do this kind of work? There are mediums and psychics who are able to supply this information, but here again, you must be very careful about who you ask. The astrological chart is particularly useful because it provides an objective description of the life task. However, you must find not only a capable astrologer but one who can sense your level of development. Astrologers capable of doing this are far and few between. Thus the problem of ill-prepared healers is made worse by the fact that there are so few qualified spiritual teachers and guides.

Those who are called to be spiritual teachers often set a particular challenge for themselves in their early years to create the necessary humility and compassion for their later work. These are qualities they are likely to have developed formerly, as well, through lifetimes after lifetimes of service and subjugation to others. The road to this life task is long and difficult. Those not showing evidence of compassion and humility are not likely to be sufficiently prepared for the task.

Those whose life task involves spiritual teaching or healing will also have wisdom, insight, and intuition. A channel who lacks these things should draw your concern. Just as developed channels do not need to rely on channeling to receive information, spiritual teachers do not have to rely on any psychic gifts of channeling ability to guide others; they are able to do so simply with their own intuitive insight. Be wary of those who go through elaborate rituals before obtaining an answer for you or who rely heavily on techniques for divining answers. Especially be very wary of those who claim to be able to divine answers to your questions about the future. So-called spiritual teachers who claim to be able to tell you specifically what will happen to you in the future are either charlatans or using any gifts they may have in an irresponsible way. Later, we will provide you with examples of responsible questions about one's future.

Because it takes many lifetimes to develop the ability to channel, those who are capable of doing this work are at various stages of development. The different kinds of mediums or channels that exist reflect the different levels of development of this ability. The most common is trance mediumship. This is carried out in full trance, while unconscious. Another less common type of mediumship is partial trance mediumship, which is carried out with the medium fully conscious but with mental functioning subdued. This last type of mediumship is actually more advanced than full trance mediumship. Unlike full trance, it allows the medium to be aware of what is being spoken through her. When this capability is fully developed, the medium does not interfere or modify the information any more than someone who is in full trance. Partial trance mediumship has the added advantage of placing less stress on the channel's nervous system than full trance mediumship.

Full trance mediumship is accurate and reliable as long as the medium is not in contact with a being from the lower astral planes. This is not likely to happen because at the level of full trance mediumship, the medium will have what is known as a "gatekeeper" whose task is to prevent all but those invited by the medium from speaking through her. The gatekeeper will allow a lower astral being to enter only if one requests admittance and admittance is granted by the medium. Usually the medium will be advised against this based on the status of the being. Thus once you have reached the level of being able to channel in full trance, the problem of channeling lower astral beings is no longer an issue.

The stages leading up to full trance mediumship are several. Many first start channeling via automatic writing, which is a form of very early channeling. It is similar to the ouija board in that it provides a tool to assist in channeling. It is not much safer than the ouija board, because it too sends a signal that you are willing to talk but may not have the development to contact higher intelligences. Automatic writing, like the ouija board, is another technique for communicating with the unseen realms that we advise strongly against because of its tendency to attract lower astral beings.

The first stage of channeling is the ability to hear words and phrases while meditating. This stage can last several lifetimes before it develops into the next one, which is the ability to hear a few sentences at a time. This stage may also last several lifetimes before developing into the next one, which is just an extension of this ability to hear longer and longer messages. Since each stage may last several lifetimes, you must not expect all that you hear to be reliable if you are receiving only bits and pieces. It is really not until one develops the ability to channel in full trance that channeling becomes reliable. Thus anyone without mediumistic capabilities— the ability to channel trance— should not be engaged in working with others nor should they assume the information they are receiving is from a reliable source.

At the point of being able to channel several paragraphs, the individual may begin to develop full trance channeling, if other factors allow this. As noted before, certain lessons must be accomplished before one is allowed to progress to this phase, because as a full trance channel, one begins to be able to use this ability to serve others. At this stage, "channeling" becomes "mediumship" (although these words are often used interchangeably), meaning that the individual's nervous system and spiritual development have progressed to the point of being able to incorporate the energy of another being into the body, allowing for the manipulation of the body and the vocal chords. Mediumship is mysterious only because it is not understood and because it does not fit with your current paradigm.

Mediumship is a fact of life. It has always existed, and it will continue to exist, because it serves a distinct purpose for the physical plane. The ego and the rational mind are necessary for physical plane functioning, but they prevent access to other planes of reality and to former lives. This is as it should be in the early stages of evolution, because much of the work of the early lives is involved with evolving the human form, the emotions, and the mind. However, there comes a time in human evolution when contact with the supernatural is appropriate. This time comes during the Old cycle when the major focus shifts to the rediscovery of oneself as a spiritual being. At last, in the Old cycle, the ego, the emotions, and the mind begin to take a back seat to the spirit.

Channeling is a tool by which information about one's true nature and one's path can be received— it is not the goal but a means to facilitate the goal of experiencing oneself as an aspect of God. Some individuals mistake the tool for the goal, which should not be encouraged, but that is no reason to throw out the tool. Information received is often misused as well, and that is also no reason to throw out the tool. The experience of channeling not only provides information that facilitates one's spiritual growth and understanding during the Old cycle but many of the Old cycle's lesson. Thus channeling has its place, and its place is in the Old cycle.

Few individuals outside the Old cycle will find channeled material of any interest or validity. Likewise, there is no one outside the Old cycle who is able to channel information in a manner that is useful. Channeling belongs to old souls and the Old cycle.

If the purpose of channeling is to bring information to old souls to facilitate their spiritual development and understanding, this premise can be used as a guideline for evaluating channeled material. Channeled material should provide general understanding about the workings of the universe and the lessons of physical plane existence; and it should provide guidance to assist you in living close to the soul's Plan without interfering with your freedom to determine the specifics of this Plan.

Everyone's life is made up of things that can be molded by one's will and things that cannot. The soul's Plan will sometimes make itself apparent through those things over which you have no control. The soul's Plan for each individual is a *general* Plan set forth prior to birth as a guideline for accomplishing certain lessons and a life task. Each person proceeds in his life on the basis of choice, while being intuitively guided along the general path mapped out by the Plan. When the person veers from the path, a sign may be introduced in the life by the soul as a means for setting him back on the path. This general path has room for many variations and choices within it; there is nothing predestined about it except the general goal. Whether the person reaches the general goal chosen prior to life and how he does so is entirely up to him. Thus each life is an interweaving of the soul's Plan with what the individual is creating each moment of his existence with his choices.

Channeling is capable of revealing the soul's Plan via communication with a being who is able to communicate with the Higher Self and the guides of the individual. The Higher Self, or soul, is that part of the individual that devises the Plan and oversees its unfolding. However, it is necessary for the Higher Self to work within the context that has been created by the individual's choices. The soul must "play it by ear," weaving the Plan and its lessons into the fabric of life the individual is creating.

It is impossible for the specifics of an individual's life to be known ahead of time, because the specifics are dependent, in large part, upon the choices that he makes, which are truly free choices—they are not predestined in any way, or they would not serve the important function they do in the evolution of the individual. Since one's future changes as quickly as it takes to change one's mind, it is difficult to predict the future with any accuracy.

When an event is already set in motion by choices made in the past, it can be predicted by psychics or those like ourselves, but it always stands the chance of being interrupted by someone's free will. If the choices change drastically, the future will also change. The future is truly fluid, always fluctuating according to the choices being made by those involved in that aspect of the future. Based on this understanding, it is important to realize that information received about the future may no longer hold true even after only a short while. The lack of understanding about this has caused some to conclude that material they received was false, when it may have been an accurate representation of the probable future.

An interesting twist to this is that information of any kind may influence someone's choices thus changing the future. Consequently, we are required to follow certain rules in providing information and guidance. One of these is that we are not to give any information that will unduly influence the current choices unless it helps set the person back on course. As you can imagine, adhering to this principle calls for wisdom and insight; no one can ever be certain how someone will respond to a message. On the other hand, if information will facilitate the soul's Plan and it has not been requested, we may ask for permission to deliver it. Delivering information is not really our goal as much as facilitating the soul's Plan and bringing further understanding about this Plan to the individual.

Past life information requires particular caution, because it cannot be verified by the individual and it can easily be misused by the ego. Those who are told they performed great deeds in a former life may react in the current life with arrogance or laziness, which can prevent them from living fully in the present. Similarly, if someone is told they must make amends for an error committed in the past, they may be immobilized by feelings of shame and hopelessness, which may jeopardize their lessons and life task. On the other hand, explaining the reason to someone, for instance, why they may be feeling responsibility to another may be somewhat relieving. Judgment on how to handle these matters is made by consulting with the individual's spirit guide who knows him better than any other and who is better able to predict his responses. However, sometimes mistakes in judgment are made. In these cases, we seek to right the mistakes as best we can given our limitations. If the situation warrants it, it is often possible to bring the individual in for another reading for this purpose, although this is not often done.

Individuals will often ask questions whose answers may not be in their best interest to receive. We usually explain this to them when this happens. Most people accept this, but some use this as a reason to disregard what we have to say, claiming we are unable to give the information they seek. Some of them seek others who will give them what they desire, even if it is not in their best interest to have it. Although inappropriate information is not given intentionally, because those who channel in full or partial trance do not usually channel lower astral beings, sometimes it will be given mistakenly out of ignorance. Mistakes are made in judgment, and they are made more frequently by those on the higher astral plane than on our level. Anyone requesting information from even a reputable medium must be aware of the possibility of receiving information that may not be helpful to them in the long run. This

is one reason why formulating appropriate questions is so important.

To return to the question at the head of this chapter, trance
mediumship is the point in the development of a channel that
marks the beginning of being able to use this ability with some
confidence. Like each of the previous stages of development, this
one will take many lifetimes before it evolves into partial trance
mediumship, the final stage. The full-trance stage is particularly
crucial to the medium's development, because it is at this point that
her soul will decide whether or not to continue pursuing the development of this ability in future lives. Although everyone has the
potential to be a medium, not everyone becomes a medium, just as
not everyone becomes a nuclear scientist. Most who choose to
pursue development of this ability do so to serve.

The choice to pursue this work entails certain considerations.
For one thing, it must be determined if the individual is suited for
this kind of work. Secondly, it must be decided if he or she can best
serve in this way, given the likely context of future lives. There
have been periods in your planet's history, such as recently, when
mediumship has not been particularly useful because of the general
disposition towards it. The current time, however, is ripening into
one that is more receptive to channeled information, and the
future time as well is likely to make good use of those with this
ability. There are a number of people who have chosen to pursue
this ability, knowing full well that there would come a time on
your planet when it would be embraced and used for the good of all.

There are also a few people who have chosen to pursue this
ability as a means for promoting themselves and gaining the
recognition they crave. They make up a small minority of mediums, but, do much to give mediumship a bad name. Those engaged
in this for their own profit, however, will be faced with balancing
this choice at some future point in time. Abuse of power is their
greatest sin, and this abuse is usually balanced most efficiently by
the experience of being totally dependent on the good will of others.
This scenario usually develops one's compassion and appreciation
of the significance of using one's power appropriately.

The stage of full trance mediumship is also significant in terms
of its lessons for the medium. It is the most dramatic of the forms
mediumship takes, because the medium's consciousness is actually
supplanted by another's. The medium is transformed more dramatically than in partial trance, because physical control is given
up to the being speaking through him. This is not the case in
partial trance channeling where the medium remains consciously
present but passive. Thus in full trance mediumship, the gestures,
facial expressions, and vocal intonations are true to the being who

is speaking through him; while in partial trance mediumship, the medium can influence, through suppression or through his own expression, the expression of the words and the physical gestures. Some view this as a drawback of partial trance channeling, but its benefits far outweigh its disadvantages. Exactness in the delivery of the message in terms of expression is not nearly as important as correct replication of the message itself, which is not affected by the passive presence of the medium. Furthermore, what one gains in health for the medium far outweighs the disadvantage of some distortion in expression of the message.

Perhaps the most obvious lesson for mediums at this stage is related to the experience of being set apart— either as one who is special or as one who is somehow bad or insane. With many, there is no middle ground in terms of their reactions to the phenomenon of mediumship. Mediums must learn to accept the varying responses with grace and be neither attached to the respect nor discouraged by the aspersions of others. The inability to do this weeds out many an individual who is channeling for the wrong reasons or not ready or not well suited to it. Dealing with other realms requires a strong sense of self; those who are easily swayed by the opinions of others stand the risk of being duped or allowing others to make choices for them. In this stage, giving one's power away can take the form of being unduly influenced by either someone's admiration or their disgust.

A number of new experiences come at this stage of development. Each time a medium's consciousness leaves her body, it explores realms formerly unknown to her. After such an experience, it becomes easier for her to know herself as an energy beyond the personal self. Furthermore, the words of support, wisdom, and insight from these realms can help her move beyond the fear and grasping of the ego. Actual contact with the energy of the being that is channeled can also serve to lift the medium into a higher state of consciousness and into an experience of the spirit, which can then be used as a model for future experiences of spirit through meditation. At this stage of development, it becomes obvious to the medium that an energy beyond herself is in operation in the universe to which her own ego cannot lay claim. She learns to distinguish between her personal self and the greater self that she experiences during these times when she is uplifted, and humility arises from this understanding.

The first stage of full trance mediumship is heralded by certain pressures and tensions in the head area upon inviting another to speak through you. It may take numerous attempts before introduction of the being can be accomplished, with each attempt resulting in tension pressure. This stage does not usually last very long and is often accomplished in a few sittings, after which the being is able to enter. You must be developed to the level of being able to do this, however, or no amount of sitting will make it possible. The medium is usually told by her guide when it is possible to do this, how to accomplish it, and what to expect. If you are not approached with this information, it is safe to assume that you are not ready. However, you can always ask; and if you receive a positive response, it can be tried. There is no harm in trying; nothing can befall you at this stage, contrary to common belief.

The worst thing that can happen is that you allow a lower astral being to speak through you rather than a higher one. This is no disaster; most mediums have experienced this. The beings who speak through you cannot hurt you or cause you to hurt yourself or others— not even when you are unconscious— because they do not have the strength to do so. The belief in possession is superstition. What is commonly known as possession usually describes one form of mental illness or another and is not possession at all. The only instance of possession, which occurs rarely, is in the case of a medium who becomes mentally unstable and who no longer has the ego strength to prevent possession by lower astral beings. It is very rare for an old soul, such as a medium, to become this de-ranged or to choose this as a life experience. Even in these rare instances, any detrimental action she might take would be more a result of her deranged mind than of the being whose consciousness is possessing her. Because possession cannot be maintained for long periods of time and because lower astral beings can manipu-late the body very little, these incidents, when they occur, are short-lived and relatively harmless. Furthermore, most beings on the astral plane, although they may be unevolved and childish, rarely seek to cause substantial harm. Your movies have grossly distorted the reality of this situation to the detriment of the majority of others like ourselves who are here to serve those on the physical plane. Hopefully, a better understanding of this type of mediumship will allay some of the fears and superstitions sur-rounding it.

In full trance mediumship, the consciousness of the medium leaves the body and travels elsewhere. It may remain in the same room or it may travel to distant planets or other realities. Where it goes and what it experiences during these times of trance depend on what the soul wants to accomplish for the medium. Some mediums are given helpful insights. Others, merely remain with those re-ceiving the reading and observe the proceedings. While some mediums are able to hear the proceedings, some are not, depending on the development of the medium.

When the consciousness of the medium is disengaged, the body remains passive, as if it is asleep, allowing the being to move it for the purpose of enhancing the understanding of the message being delivered. Moving the body requires a great deal of energy and practice on the part of the being who is doing the talking. Many beings do not have the capabilities of speaking clearly through the medium, much less moving the body effectively. The more evolved the being and the more practice he has had, the better able he is to do this. It is understandable, then, how very difficult it would be for an undeveloped being on the lower astral to cause any actual damage on the physical plane. Beings of higher intelligence have no desire to use the body for any purpose other than to facilitate the delivery of their message, and a few hand gestures will accomplish this. There is usually no reason to stand, or pace, or make any larger hand movements than those that normally accompany conversation, although there are beings who choose to present themselves more dramatically in order to make a point.

Once entrance is possible, the being must learn to manipulate the facial muscles, mouth, and larynx in order to produce speech. The being must accustom himself to each new individual he speaks through, and this can take anywhere from two or three sessions to months of practice, depending on the being's previous experience. Those who have never spoken through someone will be tutored by those who have. The medium and those listening are not aware of this, of course, but the results of this tutelage will be evident in the effectiveness of the message and how it is presented.

How a message is delivered in the beginning stages of working with a new medium can be very different from how it will be delivered after some practice. One of the major differences will be in the speed of delivery, which is likely to be much slower in the initial stages. Another difference is likely to be noted in the carriage of the head. It takes a good deal of energy and practice to be able to maintain the head in an upright position and control its movement while speaking. What often happens in the initial sessions is that the head will roll from side to side to some extent or rest upon the back of a chair for support. The sound of the voice may also be quite different until more proficiency is acquired. These are the changes that can be expected as a being becomes accustomed to a medium and to channeling in general. The more experienced being will be able to stand and move around, but this requires considerable energy from the medium and from the being and is not particularly recommended unless it serves a distinct purpose.

When the being exits, the body will go limp and the medium's consciousness will return within seconds. There are some dangers that are worth noting during this transition. First of all, because the head will temporarily lose its support, it may need to be supported for a brief moment until the medium regains control of it. Secondly, if the withdrawal happens too suddenly—as caused by a loud noise or a blow to the medium—the being will meet with discomfort and disorientation. The medium who experiences sudden and unprepared withdrawal may suffer from nausea, dizziness, headache, and depletion of energy. This is best avoided by preparing the environment so that it is free from sudden loud noises, unexpected outbursts from participants, animals that may create surprise, or other potentials for disruption. The participants should be made aware of the importance of not making surprising sounds or movements, and especially of not touching the medium with any force.

Because the beings that mediums work with vary in their evolvement and understanding, their messages vary; but for the most part, they should convey understanding and insight. The message should remain general and avoid specifics about the person's past lives, present life, and future lives. Generally, the communications are led by questions, because this format is the least likely to interfere with an individual's free will. The practice of addressing questions rather than presenting an unstructured message is a safe one and somewhat of a rule here, although there are exceptions to doing this. For instance, if a question that we feel is important is not asked, we will suggest it or request permission to comment on it. When this is the case, we proceed carefully and speak only in general terms unless questioned more specifically by the individual.

Information is not given that is deemed harmful in any way. That is why it is a rarity for information about one's death, an illness, or some other tragedy to be given. There is no value in forewarning someone about an impending event whose outcome cannot be influenced. If you receive information of this type, you should be highly suspicious of its source. If we see that someone is creating a problem that could be arrested by making other choices and we are asked about it, we will comment in a way that does not induce fear or feelings of powerlessness.

The reading itself can last anywhere from a few minutes to an hour. After this point, it is advisable for the medium to resume consciousness and take a break. Proceeding beyond an hour and a half places the nervous system of most mediums under a strain. We recommend that mediums not exceed an hour except in very special circumstances, because a depleted nervous system can lead to fatigue, listlessness, depression, loss of memory, lack of concentration, and nervous disorders such as insomnia and anxiety. In addition, it makes sense for mediums to be paid adequately for their services, especially when they involve full trance channeling, which is the most wearing.

Full trance mediumship is still the most common method of communication with the unseen realms. In the future, however, you will see increasingly more partial trance mediums, and understanding about this type of mediumship will be more widespread. Currently, the opinion is that partial trance channeling must be less advanced or somehow less trustworthy than full trance channeling, which is not the case. This impression is accounted for by two factors. One is that partial trance channeling is less common and less understood, and the other is that it is generally a less dramatic display of the phenomenon of mediumship. It is less dramatic, because the channel's consciousness remains present and does have an effect, albeit minor, on the delivery of the message. In this world full of superstition and ignorance about mediumship, partial trance mediumship has the advantage of delivering information in a less shocking form, making it more palatable to a greater number of people. Because it does not have the impact that full trance channeling does, a move to more partial trance channeling is likely to be a step along the road to greater acceptance of mediumship and an increased openness to the wide variety of information available from other realms. The amount of information available via this method of communication is exhaustive, and every area of life could benefit from opening these channels (pardon the pun) of communication.

There is one drawback to partial trance channeling which occurs only in the transition phase between full and partial trance channeling. During this transition phase, there is a possibility of interference with the message until the medium learns to remain passive and to depress her own emotional reactions and thought processes, which can only be accomplished through practice.

The kind of interference most likely to occur is that of slowing down the delivery of the message and inserting a word here or there. The insertion of words does not often change the message, because the inserted words are usually synonymous with the actual word. The worst that is likely to occur is that the opposite of what was meant is said by inserting or omitting a negative. If this happens, it is usually corrected in the next few sentences. Unfortunately, when this happens, it tends to undermine the confidence of those listening which is one disadvantage of this form of channeling. As the medium becomes more adept at remaining passive— and this can take anywhere from a few sessions to several months— mistakes become far less common. The fact that mistakes are made from time to time only attests to the medium's humanity and is no cause for disregarding the message in totality.

Partial trance channeling is simpler than full trance channeling. Preparation for all types of channeling involves a quieting of the mind, body, and emotions; and a silent invitation to the being to enter. But because less energy is needed to support the body in partial trance channeling, the medium need not be as quieted as for full trance channeling for sufficient energy to be incorporated. It is possible to accomplish the step of quieting in a matter of seconds for partial trance channeling if the medium is not unduly aroused, whereas this step may take anywhere from a few minutes to fifteen or twenty minutes for full trance channeling. If adequate preparation is not made before full trance channeling, the being may be unable to accomplish the necessary incorporation.

The exit is also simpler and safer in partial trance channeling, because less energy is involved. The medium is required to be still, but the exit is accomplished in seconds rather than in a minute or more as in full trance. Furthermore, the things likely to cause problems for the full trance channel— loud noises, surprises, blows, and so forth— are not a problem to the partial trance channel. For this type of channel, these environmental surprises cause no more pain or discomfort than usual.

The differences between full and partial trance channeling in terms of the message are minimal, and partial trance channeling has certain advantages. The fact that partial trance channeling requires slightly more advancement in development than full trance channeling is the reason it is not more common, not that it is inferior in any way. The issue of development at this stage is one of the medium's overall spiritual development rather than the development of her nervous system. It relates to the medium's advancement in terms of her lessons and, moreover, her ability to experience herself as spirit. The accomplishment of the lessons is usually fairly equal between both types of channels except in the beginning stages of full trance mediumship, but the ability to experience oneself as spirit may vary quite a bit from one kind of medium to the next. By the time they are able to channel in partial trance, most mediums are able to experience themselves as spirit throughout a good part of their day. This experience is one that comes and goes, but in the case of the partial trance medium, its presence is more common than its absence.

The experience of spirit becomes a living reality at this stage— a nearly constant state of consciousness that is not necessarily noted by the casual observer, although those who know people who live in this state are aware of something different about them. They appear more at peace, more in the moment, and less concerned with ego gratifications than most. They do not engage in petty gossip and are able to remain balanced and centered amidst changing circumstances around them. They do not experience constant bliss, as some might believe— this is reserved for only a handful of people who have nearly passed from the reincarnational system. Nor are they without a personality or saint-like. They have very distinct personalities, but their personalities do not take precedence over their spiritual selves. Greater understanding about the various levels of consciousness that comprise spiritual development would help to eliminate some of the misconceptions about those who are advanced spiritually.

CHAPTER III

WHY CHANNEL?

This is a good question, and one that many channels are confronted with. It is a particularly good question for channels to ask themselves, because a channel's motives should be pure and in keeping with her soul's Plan. Some people want to channel for all the wrong reasons. The first part of this chapter will examine some of these reasons, and hopefully enlighten you about your own motives for channeling.

The most common reason for wanting to channel is the desire for personal information. Yet, the potential for difficulties is always greatest when asking for information about yourself. It is difficult for even some of the best channels to receive reliable information about themselves, because their desires may distort the message. One is also far more vulnerable to flattery and manipulation with this type of information. All in all, it is best to avoid becoming overly involved in asking questions of a personal nature.

One way to avoid these difficulties is for mediums to ask their questions of other mediums. This is not necessary for everyone, however, given adequate spiritual development. Those who are fully developed stand little risk of distortion or inaccuracy. You can find out if you are developed enough not to distort the information by asking a reliable medium. This kind of reliability is usually present some time after partial trance channeling has developed, although others may ask a full trance channel questions about herself while she is in trance with reliability. Inexperienced partial trance mediums are the ones who stand the greatest chance of distorting personal messages.

Channels are vulnerable to manipulation when they ask personal questions, because their desires are so easily read on the astral plane by evolved and unevolved alike. Unevolved ones will most often reply with the answer you are hoping to hear, while those working in your highest good will use what they know you want to word the truth as they see it in a way that is sensitive to your desires without catering to them. Beings who are worthy of providing the kind of information you are asking for are capable of understanding the needs you have as a human being and presenting the information you need to hear in a sensitive and honest fashion. If you are receiving information that is presented in a hurtful, shocking, or insensitive way, this should raise some serious doubts about its legitimacy and source. Likewise, information that is exaggerated, unrealistic, or presented in an extremely flattering manner should be questioned as well. When we deliver information that is the same as what someone wants to hear, we are careful to state it very plainly, generally, and simply. Nor do we try to convince someone through repetition or superlatives. And if questioned about the truth of our information, we reply that belief is not necessary, rather that taking a defensive stance. We are not attached to whether you accept or reject the information we have to offer; that is you choice. However, beings from the lower astral may be invested in your acceptance. Any signs of attachment to continuing the relationship with you should bring into question the level of intelligence of the being to whom you are speaking.

Another danger in requesting information for yourself is that, because of your investment in it, you may misinterpret it. The answers that we and others like us give are general and nonspecific. Unfortunately, this allows some potential for misuse because so much can be read into it. This is the most common problem we face in delivering information; because once someone has left the channeling session, they are virtually on their own in terms of handling the information. What they choose to do with it is all a part of learning; nevertheless, it is important that people be educated about this danger. We are careful to present information that will not sway someone in one direction or another while he is making a specific choice. Yet so often, conclusions *are* drawn about specific choices based on what was said, because specific guidance is what the person was looking for. This is dangerous for a number of reasons. First of all, the individual may make a choice that he ordinarily would not have made, because he assumed that we indicated something we did not. Secondly, it falsely assumes that it is acceptable for someone to make specific decisions for another. This is only acceptable when the person is incapable of making such decisions himself, otherwise it is a gross violation of human rights. (You can draw your own conclusions about our view on certain political systems that make choices for its members.) And finally, it is dangerous because it is too easy for the individual to disavow responsibility for his actions. We are all responsible for our actions. We are responsible for delivering information to you, but you are responsible for what you do with it.

Another difficulty with requesting information about yourself may be your motive for doing so. It may be that you are seeking information for purposes of avoiding life or feeling special. Many come to us in hopes of hearing that they are special or set apart from others in some way. This would give them permission to live in terms of some ideal potential rather than in their current reality, faced with their current issues. They try to use any information they get as a means of escaping life rather than as a source of hope. Providing hope is one of the things we do best, but we do it in a way that is grounded in the current reality of the individual. Those who want to hear that they are from another planet, that they have special gifts, that they will be the one to find the cure to cancer, are more often than not disappointed with what we tell them, for it brings them back to reality. Some respond by disregarding what we have to say altogether and continuing their escapist tendencies in another form or by seeking someone else who will tell them what they want to hear. Eventually, they will have to face their problems. We try to help them see this earlier rather than later, but not everyone's eyes are ready to be opened. If we do have something very positive to say, we either say it in an unconspicuous way or we withhold it, if it seems that the person might mishandle it. As a rule, glowing acknowledgements will not be made by higher intelligences except under the rarest of circumstances, and those who are seeking this are the least likely to receive it.

Others want to channel, not to obtain information about themselves, but to obtain information about others. This desire may come under the guise of wanting to help others, but more often, those who desire such information are blatant and forthright about why they want it. They may feel they have a right to know— as in the case of parents— or they may simply feel there is no harm in obtaining information about others without their consent. In a sense, they want to use us as an eavesdropping device so that they can better control the outcome of a certain situation. We never serve this purpose; it is patently against our rules, but there are those on the lower astral who will obligingly try to provide such information— not that they can. This use of channeling would be an invasion of the human right to privacy, which we honor. We would be meddling in the most devious of ways if we passed on specific information about others to those who are merely curious.

That is not to say that we do not pass on information about others at all, but several things are taken into consideration. For one thing, we note the motive of the individual. If it is selfish, we will not be an accomplice. If it is pure, if doing so will be for the good of all, and if it is relevant to do so, we will share *general* information about another. Under no circumstances do we tell someone specifically what another is thinking, has done, or will do. There is a certain amount of judgment involved in determining what is correct and not correct according to our rules, but for the most part it is clear to us how to proceed, because the questioner's motives are so apparent to us. Were we to misuse our abilities and break this rule, we would incur considerable karma, because we are far beyond the point of knowing better, and to do this would be outright defiance of a basic rule. We are not tempted to transgress this rule, but those on the lower astral have no qualms about saying anything that will further their position. Engaging in this kind of espionage certainly incurs karma for them, but their level of evolvement is taken into consideration when the karmic balancing is assigned. Receiving information of this type is a sure sign that you have contacted a lower astral being and not a higher one. We often reply to those seeking answers to these types of questions that it is none of their business, which clearly makes our point.

Another reason some want to channel is to receive information that will benefit them in some way. They want to win the lottery, make money in the stock market, know when their rich uncle Harry will die, locate buried treasure, and on and on. People will be given answers to these types of question if doing so will benefit their growth and if the information is accessible. This can be the means by which a karmic jackpot is delivered, but this is not commonplace. If we are to perform this function and we do not ordinarily have access to the information, we will be given it. Usually, if asked such questions, we have to rely on our own judgment about whether or not to deliver the information if we have it.

Even if specific answers cannot be given, there is usually something that we can say besides the common reply, "It is not for you to know this." In the case of an uncle dying, we might say, "He is not long for this plane" or "It will be some time before he departs, there is still some work to be accomplished." In the case of a lottery, we might say, "Your chances of winning are the same as any other's" or "Your chances of winning will be better in the spring." We rarely name specific stocks, but if asked about a particular stock, we might comment. We do give information about what we see as general future trends, which can be helpful for investors. And although we do not tell someone how to invest or how much to invest, we will answer specific questions about this as best we can unless we feel that it would somehow be detrimental to the individual's growth, in which case, we offer advise about what he needs to focus on for himself. As far as guiding individuals to lost or buried treasure, if we have access to this information, and we might, we may give a clue to its whereabouts or confirm one's suspicions about it, but rarely would we offer detailed information on these matters. We do not believe it is a proper use of our energies to make things easy for people; they must be in the world in an ordinary way without special help from us.

Another motivation for channeling is to receive comfort, support, and friendship. Comfort and support can be found in these communications and we do not find it inappropriate to provide this. Some people, however, try to extend the comfort and support we offer to friendship, which is not appropriate, because it is too easy to have us as friends—we do not demand anything, we are always supportive, and we do not need comforting. Friendship is not this kind of one-way street; it is a give and take with clashes of opinion and life style. This way of relating to us is never encouraged, although those on the lower astral plane prefer this kind of relationship. If you are in need of a friend, you must find one elsewhere. In not serving this purpose, we are not placing ourselves above you, for we are not parents to you either, which is another need some people have.

People who are looking for a parent are looking for someone to depend on, someone to tell them what to do. We encourage these individuals to depend on themselves and to make their own choices, which is actually what a good parent would do anyway. Dependency can be a problem, and when it is, we provide counseling and do what we can to discourage it. Some individuals may even be advised to stop consulting these realms to help them learn to rely on their own instincts and intuitions. There usually comes a time when they are ready to relate to us in a more centered way, as equals.

It seems to be a rare individual who does, in fact, relate to us as the equals that we are. Because you are subject to the perceptions of the physical plane, most of you are not immediately aware of your likeness to us. We are, in fact, one and the same, but no amount of discourse can bring this awareness to you. Meditation is a very important practice for everyone, but especially for those involved in communication with us. Because one gains a respect for oneself and one's place on the universe through meditation by experiencing one's own being, it is the single most important step you can take in creating a balanced relationship with us.

The fact that many people approach channeling for all the wrong reasons does not mean that channeling cannot be used for good. There are many good reasons for channeling, not the least of which is to gain useful information, especially that which is not readily available to you. That is not to say that we never offer information that is already available to you. But, we do not allow ourselves to be used as an encyclopedia, and if individuals can get answers to what they are looking for from the usual sources, we direct them to those sources. The kind of information that we are able to provide that people are likely to find most useful relates to the unseen realms, to what you consider the paranormal, and to those things that lay as yet undiscovered by you. Suggestions and advice are also forthcoming from us when asked, and this is another type of information.

One of the most common and beneficial uses of channeling has been to impart information regarding health. Edgar Cayce is the most well-known medical medium, but there have been others. Channeling has been used for diagnosis, prognosis, and treatment as well as for prevention. Specialists are called upon in the astral realm and beyond to address questions of this nature. There are instances when an illness or difficulty is not treatable for karmic reasons; illness is frequently used by the soul to teach needed lessons. When this is the case, standard treatment may be ineffectual until the lesson is accomplished, causing some confusion in the medical community as to why remedies work for some but not for others.

On the other hand, there are many illnesses that are treatable but whose cure is as yet unknown to you. This is an area in which we can be of great benefit to humanity, although specific answers will not often be given. What usually will be offered are suggestions or clues about where to search for the cure, because simply giving answers would not allow for the human mind to exercise itself. Medical guides can also help by confirming or disagreeing with current medical diagnoses and treatments and by offering suggestions for treatment. Sometimes, guides will even suggest remedies used long ago that are no longer commonly in use, but the ingredients may be difficult to find and identify by names given by the guide who may not be familiar with updated nomenclature. Information and treatment suggestions are also available for mental illness, an area that for you is yet in its nascence in terms of understanding and treatment.

Channeling can also provide useful information concerning your planet: its weather; the changes that have occurred and will occur to its surface; its place in the universe; its geographical and human history; and human, animal, plant, and planet origins and evolution.

Another fruitful area of inquiry is that of spiritual understanding. Answers can be received to philosophical and religious questions as well as to those pertaining to spiritual evolution or to one's personal spiritual progress. We will present such information from our perspective and in a way that is most understandable to you, which is not always easy.

Information about the soul's Plan is helpful in assisting people to accept the Plan and live within it. At the same time, when these questions are answered, it becomes apparent to people that the Plan is general and largely dependent upon their own creation. Many people have the mistaken belief that their lives are planned down to the last detail, which is far from the reality. The Plan is very general; we cannot emphasize this enough. Nevertheless, there is a Plan and straying from it may result in difficulties. Some difficulties are the soul's attempt to steer a person in a certain direction, others are part of his lessons, while still others are the result of poor choices. Insight into why you may be experiencing difficulties and what you can do to ameliorate or learn from them is available from other realms.

Information concerning your life task, what you have chosen to accomplish in this particular life, can also be obtained. Sometimes the life task involves releasing a certain karmic debt or pattern of behavior from the past, and sometimes it involves accomplishing a specific task or developing a specific talent. Whatever, the case, you can receive a general idea of what it entails. If others will be involved in it, when it is likely to culminate, if it is likely to be completed in this life, and other information that would facilitate its accomplishment without interfering with your freedom to choose its specific course.

We and others like ourselves will also will provide you with our opinions about politics in general and in specific, commenting on your current political leaders and their policies from what we understand to be higher perspective. Perspective is often needed in politics, for too often short-range solutions are accepted, rather than making a commitment to future needs.

Insight and understanding about current social concerns are also offered from other realms when requested. Just as the many social issues you face today are a result of past social policies and choices, the social issues of tomorrow will be a result of your current choices. You can overcome your current social ills simply by understanding what factors contributed to them and by making choices that would better serve your goals.

Causes are never simple, however; there are always numerous contributing factors which affect each other. We and others like us are able to analyze these causative factors for you and make suggestions for future actions based on our own experience with human history. You are not the only civilization that has had criminal difficulties, drug problems, and homeless people. You are not the only civilization that has experienced a growing gap between the rich and the poor and its resulting tension. And you are not the only civilization that has failed to care adequately for the young, the old, and the mentally and physically incapacitated. We are able to take all factors in a situation into account, analyze them, and evaluate the various solutions. It is not that we say, "Do this, and your problems will disappear;" it is never that simple, straightforward, or certain. But, we *are* able to make highly educated suggestions based on a larger information base than you may have access to.

Another fruitful area of inquiry is that of science and technology. Although science has brought great advancements to society, it has lacked perspective and ethical guidelines, resulting in major abuses of the creative ability. Because something *can* be done through science, should it be done? This question has never been adequately addressed, leaving scientists to do what they may and others to worry about the consequences. We must stand responsible for each and every choice we make in life. This is no less true for scientists, who are continually deciding in what directions to place their creative energies. It is not only society that pays the price for ill-placed creative energies, but the scientists themselves. It is possible for them to accrue considerable karma if their creations do not serve the good of all because of greed, desire for fame, or ignorance. The fact that we and others like ourselves are able to shed light on the ethical and long-range ramifications of certain creations makes our availability to scientists particularly useful. Ultimately, they must decide how to use their energies, but information about how their creations are likely to impact on the world can be obtained from other realms.

Although creative ideas are not offered outright, pieces of an idea from which to work may be. We are also not allowed to give solutions to your problems, such as your energy problem, not only because it would be too easy but because it might interfere with human evolution. We are reminded of the importance of this precept by others who failed to follow it in the past. Information was given to the now famous continent of Atlantis that they were not prepared to handle and which they promptly used to destroy themselves. A grievous misjudgment was made in divulging this information at the time. The repercussions from this disaster are still being felt in ways that are not even known by you. This misjudgment incurred a karmic responsibility on the part of the beings involved to assist and guide the earth more responsibly, which they are fulfilling today under the guidance of others.

Works of art, music, and other forms of creative expressions also must originate from the intuition rather than from channeling. We are channeling this book now as a means of conveying information, but it is hardly art. We would not channel a novel, for instance, or poetry without taking full credit for it. Thus creative products from other realms must receive appropriate acknowledgement of their origin; it would be unfair for a person to lay claim to something he did not create. Furthermore, this would short-circuit the learning entailed in the creative process.

Besides information, suggestions, and advise, channeling can offer support and encouragement. However, we do not give encouragement or support when it is not due or if it seems that doing so will result in a negative effect, such as bragging, laziness, or arrogance; and it is not given in glowing or exaggerated terms. Encouragement is most often given when needed and rarely when it does not serve an immediate function. Our encouragement comes less in the form of direct statements such as, "You are doing well" and more in the form of insight, by pointing out what is being gained from a particular experience and how it fits into one's Plan. This is usually a more powerful form of support than compliments or platitudes. That is not to say that we never compliment individuals who are unaware of the fine job they are doing, but we find that this is only so helpful. People must ultimately come to see, through understanding, that their experiences have value and are leading them to greater love. This kind of spiritual upliftment and understanding is the most unique thing we have to offer. This kind of information is not available from any other source except intuitively, so offering perspective and understanding is one of our most important functions and one of the best reasons for channeling.

Along with this perspective may come information about past lives. It is only in the service of this overall perspective that past life information is offered, however, for nothing is ever offered that does not immediately serve the purpose of furthering one's understanding and the accomplishment of one's current lessons and life task.

One of the most difficult tasks we and others like ourselves perform is retrieving past life information. It is not widely understood—but it should be—that reading the Akashic records requires a high level of ability. Those on the higher astral plane are in the process of developing this ability, so any information received from them pertaining to past lives must be accepted with this in mind. We are usually able to perceive the information we need for others, but there are times when we make mistakes. Psychics who claim to read the Akashic records are many, but few are capable of doing so with true accuracy. We suggest that you seek past life information from those beyond the higher astral plane and not from psychics at all. Guides from the higher astral are able to give accurate guidance about the soul's Plan and some past life information, but it may be necessary to speak directly to the guide of the particular individual for whom you wish information. Other higher astral beings may not be able to offer accurate past life information about people whom they are not guiding.

Another misunderstanding about past life information is that it is assumed to be important. So much of the information about the past that can be retrieved is simply irrelevant and useless to one's current life. Lifetime upon lifetime is spent learning basic lessons and living very mundane and ordinary existences. The few lifetimes of glamour or notoriety may be equally irrelevant in terms of one's current lessons. There are usually only a few facts about anyone's past lives that are relevant, the disclosure of which would serve a purpose. Nevertheless, there is usually much curiosity about past lives and a desire to have any kind of information one can get. This attitude is not helpful, because it is a waste of time. We do not indulge these desires when it is apparent that doing so serves no purpose, and we try to educate others about our attitude, so they no longer waste their time and energies on this.

Another problematic tendency is using past life information to glorify the ego. This is one step beyond a waste of time and is actually using material to one's detriment. It is important to understand that we all must experience every aspect of life in order to develop fully: We all must be rich and poor, famous and ordinary, leaders and followers. And we all eventually develop certain talents over the course of our lifetimes worthy of bringing notoriety and wealth. To focus on only those lifetimes when you were outwardly successful is to miss the point. The point is that each lifetime is valuable; the most ordinary ones may actually benefit one's spiritual growth more than the most splendorous.

We have tried to show how channeling can be used for good or for ill. It is up to you how you will use it. For some the temptations to misuse it are too great, and they will struggle with the lessons presented here. There is a point in the struggle though; even a misuse of channeling serves a purpose in teaching certain lessons. One cannot progress in one's spiritual growth without overcoming, for instance, the tendencies of the ego to set itself apart and try to be special. Channeling is a tool for teaching some of these most difficult lessons. It is wise, when you become involved in it, to be aware that you are opening yourself up to some potentially difficult lessons. Life is not easy, and that which is of value is not easily gained. What is gained as a result of these lessons is worth the struggle, confusion, and difficulties one may meet along the way. One cannot turn away from these lessons, for they must be faced by all at one time or another; and channeling is the means by which many face these lessons very dramatically. Be forewarned.

THE DANGERS OF CHANNELING

In spite of advise to the contrary, some who are not ready to channel will do it anyway. Because of the underlying need driving them, they are likely to run into trouble; and their lessons will be related to what is driving them. This section is written for those who are not developed to the level of trance channel but who, nevertheless, are using channeling in their lives. Although they should never channel for others, many of them will anyway, because they may not understand that they lack proper development.

Contributing to this problem is the difficulty in discovering how developed you are and what role channeling is to play in your life. Many undeveloped channels who ask these questions ask them unknowingly of lower astral beings who do not give them truthful answers, but rather encourage them to channel. This is how some channels get off to a bad start. Hopefully, some of you are reading this book and can save yourselves some trouble.

Our purpose is not to exaggerate the dangers of channeling. Channeling is not fatal, nor is it likely to lead to any kind of physical pain or harm. The worst dangers are more likely emotional: You can become confused, deluded, rejected, shocked, afraid, or disappointed. Keeping this in mind, let us continue with a look at the potential for harm involved in channeling.

The worst case scenario is one in which someone carries out a channeled suggestion or command to kill or harm himself or another. The most common way to receive such a message is through the ouija board or automatic writing. It is also possible to encounter malevolent spirits without these channeling aids if you have yet to receive protection from these lower astral levels, but usually someone is not able to sustain long conversations at this level of development without an aid. Of course, it is not the ouija board or automatic writing or even the spirits who are responsible for a malevolent act— although the spirits play a part in it— but the one who chooses to do it. Thus nothing that you receive from channeling is in itself harmful if one acts on the information received with discrimination and integrity. In the case of receiving malevolent suggestions, the discriminating thing to do is to cease all communication with those who make such suggestions.

It is surprising to see how easily some people trust what others say— especially others who are no longer in the body. People who fall prey to this usually have little self-respect or have been taught through an authoritarian approach to let others do their thinking for them. They may also be acting out of anger from having been abused and maybe using the spirit's direction as justification for their destructive acts. Someone need not be mentally or emotionally ill to fall prey to following another's direction— only deluded. Some spirits are able to cast such intricate and plausible webs of deceit that even a healthy individual may be deluded into seeing things the spirit's way.

Throwing out the ouija board is only a partial solution. The real solution lies in learning to trust yourself. You learn this kind of trust by making choices and learning from these to make better ones. Learning to make choices is like any other skill— it develops through practice. Those who are not allowed to make their own choices, do not learn to make good choices; they only learn to obey. Worse than that, they learn to distrust themselves.

Children should be taught that their first allegiance must be to what they feel is right rather than to what another says is right. This approach to raising children requires a belief in the innate goodness of humanity. Those who have trouble believing this need to re-examine their philosophies that contradict this premise, such as the doctrine of Original Sin. If at your core you are not of God but of the Devil, how can you trust yourself? If you cannot trust yourself, who can you trust? With a basic shift in philosophy, it is possible to raise children who know what they feel and who trust their feelings. Democracy is founded on this trust in the individual to make his own decisions and so is spiritual evolution; fostering this self-trust in your children should be a priority.

The only physical harm that can come from channeling, outside of following another's direction to physically harm oneself or another, is from over-extending oneself. Full trance mediums, and to some extent other mediums, should restrict their periods of channeling to no more than three hours daily with hourly breaks of at least one-half an hour. These are guidelines for a healthy and relatively young individual. Under stress, poor health, or agedness these guidelines change. It is best to consult your guide about your specific limitations, for they are best able to address your individual needs. Exceeding the limits runs the risk of straining the nervous system, which can have various repercussions depending on the extent of the strain and its duration. Following these cautionary measures also has the benefit of keeping the medium grounded by allowing her time for other activities and a life outside her life as a medium.

Another danger for those who indiscriminately follow advise given to them by beings incapable of proper guidance is the potential for loss of reputation and important social contacts. Even very intelligent people can fall prey to bad advise if it *appears* sensible. We know of individuals who have made drastic changes in their lives—moved, left jobs, divorced, changed careers—based on advise or information they have received from lower astral beings. The results of these changes can be devastating enough once the person discovers he was mistaken, but there may also be a loss or reputation to mend as well. After such a mistake, the person's judgment and stability may be called into question, even by close friends, which can take years to repair.

In this scenario, the damage is spiritual as well. Although an important lesson is being learned, the events may sidetrack the individual's Plan and even cause him to miss certain opportunities. Every Plan has crucial points where people and opportunities manifest. When unplanned changes occur, particularly major ones, the soul must readjust the Plan to accommodate the changes. Setting the individual back on course may take several years, and the readjustments might cause certain opportunities to be missed. In addition, there is a certain amount of karma that is accrued when someone gives away his power of choice and acts indiscriminately, and a balancing will have to occur to teach the required lesson, if further learning is necessary.

Financial loss is also a possibility when listening to poor advise. One of the reasons many seek advise from the spirit realm is to improve their financial condition. It is not unusual for people to seek advise about investments in the stock market and other business ventures. If someone is contacting a lower astral being, they are likely to get very high-blown predictions and exaggerated claims for money-making schemes. Lower astral beings are more likely to make outrageous suggestions than conservative ones, because the results from their point of view are so much more satisfying. If you were trying to make an impact on the physical plane, would you settle for something minor or would you prefer to see how far you could go (or how foolish a human being can be)? These beings are never sure if you will follow their advise or not, but it is usually worth it to them—even if they lose you as a companion—if they can get you to do something dramatic. Listening to their financial advise can lead to major losses.

Those who use a ouija board or automatic writing are more apt to establish a relationship with a particular being or a group of beings than someone who does not use these aids, simply because long conversations cannot be maintained without them when one is undeveloped. Using the ouija board or preparing to do automatic writing sends out a signal to those on the astral plane that you want to speak with someone, and they will approach you obligingly. The advantages of not using one of these aids are that you still have a chance of contacting your guide briefly before others arrive and that there are some lower astral beings who will not bother with you unless you can sustain a long conversation with them.

Contact with the lower spirit world is easy enough. One need not be a developing channel to be able to move the planchette of a ouija board, and someone who is a developing channel will be able to move it easily and quickly. This allows even the least developed channel to speak for indefinite periods of time to spirits on the lower astral plane. Many upon discovering they have the ability to do this, especially if the planchette moves easier and more quickly for them than for others, become intrigued. In the beginning, various beings are likely to vie for your attention, but eventually a certain being or group of beings will lay claim to you. At this point, they usually work to establish a trusting relationship with you. The catch is that the more you speak with them, the stronger the bond becomes between you, especially when it is nourished with compliments, encouragement, and information you want to hear. An attachment and loyalty develop which can be quite strong, and the potential for emotional pain is born.

Others working the ouija board may become equally engaged, but sometimes they act as skeptics, which is healthy for the ones who are not equally discriminating. One of the advantages to the ouija board over automatic writing is that there is at least an opportunity for others to be involved who can act as skeptics for those who are too ready to believe.

Automatic writing has the disadvantage of being a "closet" activity. Because of the stigma attached to it, people will engage in it secretly and may become very enmeshed with those they are speaking to before anyone else is even aware that this is going on. The secrecy serves to preserve the channeling relationship for long periods of time, which in many cases, can be very undermining of one's other relationships.

What makes these relationships so confusing and deluding is that it is possible to receive very substantial information on a variety of topics. Usually, however, this information is the kind you could find in any library. This activity would be relatively harmless if the relationship remained on this level, but it never does. Other more personal information is invariably introduced about past lives, what friends are thinking and saying, what will happen in the future to Uncle Freddy, and so forth. Since you have no way of verifying this type of information, you may accept it along with the more educational information. Even if the one channeling does not ask personal or future-oriented questions, spirits will invariably offer this information, because this is how they have their fun. If the channeling relationship were to remain on an educational level, these kinds of spirits would eventually lose interest and leave.

The real danger lies in receiving personal information and advice, especially about the future. You would not go to a dentist for advise about your feet, so why go to a baby— in evolutionary terms— for advise about your life? No one does this intentionally, of course. Knowing that the greatest danger lies in getting personal information can help those dealing with these realities to avoid some pain. If you are determined to channel and unsure who you are contacting but do not accept any information about yourself or those close to you, you will probably have a relatively innocuous experience.

The reason there can be so much pain involved in relationships with lower astral beings is not only that they wreak havoc with people's lives with their bad advise, but that they also betray their trust and affection. Those who have come to depend on such a relationship for comfort, support, companionship, and assistance are devastated when the relationship is suddenly found to be built on false grounds. Some individuals are so distraught at the thought of losing the kindness and support they have been receiving that they accept the excuses or forgive the being's mistakes and continue the relationship. A relationship like this, however, is bound to come tumbling down sooner or later. The sooner the better, for the longer it drags on, the more painful the eventual betrayal.

There are a number of ways someone might find out that they have been betrayed. The most common way is for the spirit to make a mistake in predicting something. Spirits will always try to gloss over their mistakes and make excuses, but anyone with the least bit of discrimination is likely to be alarmed by this, especially if it has happened repeatedly. Discovery comes next, commonly as a result of someone else intervening and suggesting that something is not right. Often what is evident to others is not evident to the one doing the channeling because of the investment they have in continuing. They need the objectivity of others to show them their mistake in judgment. On the other hand, sometimes the individual himself feels suspicious and confronts the spirit, who confesses. Confession only happens with less tenacious spirits. If you are fortunate enough to have contacted one of these, you probably have not become overly involved anyway. Many spirits will play with people for a little while, knowing all along what they are doing is wrong, and quit when their consciences get the better of them. However, they may be very skillfully replaced by another spirit desirous of continuing the game under the same guise. You cannot count on confrontation with these beings to bring forth the truth. Sometimes it will; more often it will not.

When spirits are confronted and it is apparent to them that the charade is over, their responses are varied and not to be trusted. One response is to apologize and to try to negotiate another kind of relationship. Another response is to make fun of you for being so foolish, which is usually a last resort after trying other methods of retaining contact with you. And finally, the most ill-tempered spirits will try to scare you with threats, saying they will never leave and that they will drive you crazy until you commit suicide. The most horrible threats you can imagine have been used at one time or another. There is not a single spirit who has ever been able to carry out a threat. They have no power but that which you give them.

Needless to say, after such an encounter—whether you are pleaded with, mocked, or threatened—there is a sense of shame, anger, hurt, and loss. One of the hardest things about this kind of betrayal is the loss of friendship or mentor, that you thought you had. The loss is real, as real as if it had been an actual person who betrayed you and left. Many go through a period of grieving after such a discovery. It is not uncommon for those who have been actively involved with spirits in long-term relationships to plunge into a period of depression; the loss coupled with the sense of shame and foolishness, possibly compounded by mocking and nasty threats, can be difficult to bear. Those who have been given grandiose predictions, making them feel infallible and above the common everyday human concerns, suddenly, have to face the fact that they are human after all. A discovery which involves this much deception can be devastating indeed; one's hopes for the future are dashed, and one is faced with the wreckage remaining in one's life.

CHAPTER IV

HOW TO CHANNEL

Not everyone can channel, and no amount of practice or wishing can make it so unless the necessary development exists. Those who have a strong desire to channel should examine their motives, for it is difficult to differentiate between the desire to be special and have access to information and the soul's drive to do this work. Relatively speaking, there are only a few people who have channeling as their life work; many more are simply in the development phase and should not attempt to work with others. With this said, let us continue first with an explanation of how to determine if you are ready to channel and then how, in fact, to do it.

There are as many ways this ability makes itself apparent as there are people, which explains why there are so many misunderstandings about channeling and its development. The developmental process is unique for each person and will unfold in its own unique way depending on past life experience with it and current lessons.

Some channels are born with immediate access to this ability, but it is far more common to have it develop later when the individual is ready to use it. If it is to the advantage of the life task and lessons and if it developed fully in former lives, evidence of it may show immediately. More often than not, however, a channel will have certain lessons or karmic patterns to release before she is ready to have this ability operate. For those rare individuals who begin their work as messengers at an early age, it can be very difficult, because they cannot live a normal life. Yet, sometimes this is chosen because it does make such a deep impression on others.

For those who regain their ability to channel at some point later in life, it can happen suddenly or very gradually over a number of years, depending on what is best for the channel's growth. Because of this, those with potential may not know they have it and others without it may wonder if they do. The only way to discover whether or not you have it, and what your current level of development is, is to ask a reputable medium. This is a crucial step in avoiding future difficulties and the possibility of investing your energy inappropriately.

Sometimes a channel will regain full ability without regaining the protection she once had. When this occurs, there is always a reason for it. We know of one highly developed channel who did not receive protection so she would encounter the pitfalls of the lower astral realms to prepare her to teach others about them. She was given excellent information interspersed with inaccurate personal information about the future so that she could learn these lessons. When the lessons were learned, she regained her protection. This kind of teaching goes on rather frequently to varying degrees according to what is needed. When beginning channeling, be aware that it may be used to bring you the lessons you need.

There are a number of indicators of a channel's readiness to do this work. A strong desire to gain understanding about broad topics and to serve others through imparting this information is an indication that channeling may possibly be your life work. However, it is easy to fool yourself in these matters, and you must be starkly honest about your motives for channeling. Another indication of readiness is non-attachment to receiving personal information about the future. This is evidence of a healthy attitude towards the future and an understanding of your own part in creating it. A final indication is the sense that you can do nothing *but* this, that is, that channeling is your destiny and you must live with it for good or for bad. The tendency for many is to glamorize channeling and see it as an answer to not knowing what else to do. This is naive. Those who are truly ready to do this work have a realistic view of the struggles involved, the social disparagement, the financial limitations, and the limitations of channeling itself.

If you are ready to be a channel, the skill, the proper attitude, and the desire will be there. You should not attempt working with others, however, unless you are capable of channeling in full or partial trance. If you are simply receiving messages mentally, and this is the only form your channeling takes, it is not safe to assume these messages are reliable. You can use the messages received at this level for yourself with caution and discrimination, but you should not involve others by channeling information for them.

The proper attitude is another ingredient necessary to doing this work well, and one we have briefly touched upon before. It includes humility, realism, and skepticism. A properly prepared channel has the appropriate amount of skepticism and is well aware of the unpredictability of life. She must also be in a position to assist others in properly utilizing information by being in proper relation to it herself. If a channel vehemently defends the source of the information being channeled, be wary. The channel should not be attached to whether you believe the information or not, although this is easier said than done. Her attitude should be that channeling is a tool for conveying information which the receiver has the responsibility to do with as he will. This detachment from the material one channels is important, because it signifies a healthy skepticism and humility.

Humility is an indication that one is evolved enough to use this ability properly. Any flaunting of oneself and one's ability should be highly suspect. A channel with the proper attitude understands his or her position as an instrument, as well as the limitations of what she is doing. She is not impressed by the phenomenon of channeling or the possibilities it presents, because basically it is all just information. She also recognizes the fallibility and ordinariness of those in the unseen realms. This realistic attitude toward channeling and what it can and cannot do helps the channel keep her feet on the ground and actively engaged in life rather than running from it.

Along with skill and the proper attitude, the proper kind of desire is an indication of readiness to do this work. There are two kinds of desire that relate to channeling: The desire to serve and the desire to benefit from what one is doing. The channel's motive is usually glaringly apparent to others. Those who are channeling to benefit their egos, even if they are highly capable, will find that their work with others will not progress as it might, because others will be turned away by their ego-involvement. This is true for psychics and other healers as well. The gaining of humility and a true desire to serve are major steps along the path for all types of healers. There are those who are capable channels who have not as yet learned these lessons, and until they do, they are not sufficiently prepared to serve others. It is not enough to have the ability to channel, one must also have the proper attitude and the proper kind of desire.

How does one gain the proper attitude, if it is lacking? It could be gained by meeting the negative responses of others; experience eventually teaches us what we are doing wrong. Once you have determined through self-examination and consultation with a reliable medium that channeling is your life work, you are ready to ask the next question, "When will I be ready to begin?"

The answer to this question depends on whatever general life lessons and whatever other lessons around channeling remain. Usually, the greater part of one's life lessons are accomplished prior to the onset of channeling, but this is not true in all cases, depending on one's Plan. Less commonly, the life lessons and those pertaining to channeling are intertwined and unraveled in unison. Whatever the case may be, some preparation time— anywhere from a few weeks to several years, depending on what is in need of accomplishing— is usually necessary before launching this career.

For new channels, at least a year or two is needed to understand, explore, and accept this new ability and make the necessary personal adjustments.

During this preparatory period, you will have to explore how you would like to use this ability in your life. The answer to this question will determine to a large extent how you spend your time during this period. If you want to do reading for others, as many channels do, you will want to talk with other mediums and find out as much as you can about this aspect of the work. Some channels prefer to use their ability to gather information about topics of interest to them, in which case, this preparatory period is a good time to begin recording information and reading other available channeled material. Some perfectly adequate channels will choose to do neither of these things but will focus their energies, instead, on using channeling to increase their own understanding and enhancing their personal growth. Individuals interested in using it in this way are likely to be those who are working in the healing professions where personal growth and insight are paramount.

To be a good channel, it is not necessary to use channeling in this preparatory stage to learn about yourself, but using it in this way is helpful in understanding the proper changes you are likely to be experiencing and in acquiring the proper attitude needed to be a good channel. It is a rare individual who does not need some guidance and support during the first few months or years. It is not uncommon for the onset of channeling to bring about certain external changes in one's life; relationships may be shaken as may one's occupation and entire lifestyle. This may be a difficult time period not only for the channel but for those closest to her, who will wonder what this will lead to socially, financially, and personally.

When and if the time comes for you to begin to use your skills with others, you will generally be notified by your guide or teacher. However, if you are mistakenly communicating with lower astral beings, they are likely to encourage you to channel for others before you are actually ready. They will announce your readiness to you flamboyantly, with exaggerated enthusiasm and praise. With guides or teachers, the announcement comes as a simple statement and an inquiry into how you feel about doing this kind of work.

Advice about how to proceed at this point will be given by your guide if asked, but the following guidelines should help too. First of all, telling others of your ability can be very difficult for you and those close to you. Many people do not even know what channeling is or worse, they equate it with possession as presented in horror movies. There is also a sense that mediumship is sexual in some way, perhaps because it involves the incorporation of the energy of another. To some people's way of thinking, it is a metaphor for sexual union. There is no relationship to sexual union, but this idea still lingers in some people's minds, giving mediumship a negative connotation. If attitudes about mediumship would be honestly explored, their superstitious nature would be apparent. We hope to facilitate a shift in attitudes to healthier, more realistic ones so that humanity can begin to make use of channeling as the resource that it is. Nevertheless, when you approach others with the information that you are channeling, you must be prepared to meet the superstitions of others head-on.

There are more helpful and less helpful ways of dealing with the superstitions of others. For one thing, it does not help to become defensive, angry, or rejecting. Approach this challenge with understanding and compassion, as a good teacher would approach those in need of instruction. This is where ego detachment comes in handy, but it is not always easy to be personally detached from negative responses that are directed at something you value. You will simply have to understand some people, no matter what you say, will not accept your ideas.

This entire situation is best handled by not introducing the fact that you channel to anyone who does not ask about it. It is best at first to tell only those closest to you when it seems necessary to do so. Allow it to unfold from there, offering information about it only when you are asked. The establishment of oneself as a channel can be a very slow process, because it is best to have it spread as it will by word of mouth rather than by your own announcement or advertisement.

The majority of individuals will never seek your services or those of any medium. There are relatively few individuals who are or ever will be open to channeling. Although there is some hope for this changing in the future, this is not a service that has wide appeal yet. For this reason, many mediums by necessity have other forms of employment. Supporting yourself entirely by channeling can be difficult, to say the least, unless you are willing to travel from city to city throughout the year, as many do.

If you are to support yourself partially or fully in this manner, it must be approached like a business and handled in a very businesslike manner, the only difference being that you do not promote yourself in quite the same way as an ordinary business. We would not encourage you at any point to take out an ad in a newspaper naming your services. Instead, we suggest that you offer free one or two hour lecture/demonstrations. You will, of course, need to announce these in newspapers and flyers, and this will be you advertising. You will want to include what the topic or purpose will be, where and when it will take place, and information pertaining to your qualifications or background. If you do this on a regular basis—two or three times a year in every city you go to—you will find yourself becoming known by a growing minority. Nevertheless, you should expect it to take perhaps as much as a year or two before your trips to these cities are truly worthwhile. No one said this would be easy, but if you are doing this with the right intentions, immediate success and recognition will not be foremost in your mind.

It is best not to take your services to other cities until you are comfortable with yourself as a medium in your own locale. If you are not adjusted to this new image of yourself before venturing off to new places, you run the risk of appearing inexperienced and insecure, which—no matter how excellent a channel you may be—will influence how people view your work. This is another reason to allow a slow unfolding of your channeling business. You may indeed be a full-fledged medium, but there is more to succeeding in this work than having the ability to channel.

Let's talk about image. The image of the medium has been that of someone who has seances in darkened rooms, bedecked with bangles, hoop earrings, silk scarves, and exotic clothing. You can either reinforce this one by choosing to dress in this fashion or you can pick another one of your choosing. The important thing to ask yourself in pondering your outward appearance is whether or not it is consistent with how you want others to see you. If you want others to assume you fit the stereotype and you feel this serves your goals, then dress the part. However, in our opinion, a new image is needed that will not cater to people's superstitious misunderstandings about mediumship.

A new outward image for mediums can do much in the way of changing the old stereotypes; so please give careful thought about the impact your image is likely to have on the field of mediumship. We have no specific suggestions in terms of apparel, for it is important to express who you are through your own choice of clothing. We are merely suggesting that you present an image of who you are rather than who you think others expect you to be. Along these same lines, it might be helpful to point out that just because you do something unusual does not mean that you must dress in an unusual way. A more ordinary, conservative, and professional image will inspire trust as well as elevate mediumship from the realm of the occult. Please give careful consideration to your attire and to the image you present to others, just as you would in establishing yourself in any other business.

People will also draw conclusions about your competence and about mediumship in general based on how you speak and behave.

Be aware that your behavior will be watched carefully and evaluated by others, perhaps unfairly at times, but this is how it is for mediums. Because people have certain expectations and beliefs about mediums, they will watch you as if you were something divorced from the human race. They will wonder not only about your unusual ability but about your personal life as well. Unless you wish to open yourself up to scrutiny and judgment, be careful about sharing personal information with others. Being a channel is a little like being a celebrity in that people will want to know about you, but they may not use what they find out to your advantage. And as with celebrities, others may find it difficult to forget that you are a channel and relate to you in an ordinary way. Becoming a professional channel will change your life, and this is only one of the ways.

Not only will others see you differently when you begin to do this work, but you will feel differently as well. One of the benefits of this work is the acceleration of one's spiritual growth. You will be receiving energy of a higher vibration into your body each time you channel a being of higher intelligence. This energy actually works to raise your own vibrational level to a higher one. This process of accelerated growth also stirs up the emotional body, making it necessary to attend to emotional issues. Meditation will facilitate both the integration of this energy and the healing of the emotional issues that arise. The issues can be attended to in meditation simply by asking for the assistance of spirit. Many are unaware of the importance of inviting spirit to work in their lives. Unless it is invited, it operates only in accordance with what the will allows. On the other hand, if one asks spirit to do what needs to be done, it can go about its business efficiently and uninhibitedly. Not attending to these emotional issues can create difficulties later on.

You are also bound to experience more joy and peace as a result of doing this work. Through continual contact with a higher source of information, you will be reminded of the perfection of the universe and your place in it, which will help you live more peacefully with your Plan. You are also likely to notice certain habits drop away as the ego loses its grip. There will be less need for the usual ego gratifications and less time spent in search of them. Thus you are likely to find yourself engaged in different sorts of activities than before, simply because you prefer them. The kinds of activities likely to gain in appeal are walks in the woods, meditation, creative expression, meaningful conversation, listening to music, and reading inspirational literature. The kinds of activities likely to fall away are idle chatter and purposeless social activity, television watching, eating solely for the pleasure of doing so—especially foods that detract from one's health and energy— perfectionistic and obsessional behavior, and activities that aimlessly pass time. You will find yourself more present in each moment and less focused on the past and on the future. These changes come about slowly in most cases, but there are instances of rather dramatic transformation as a result of becoming involved in this work. You need not be concerned about losing something as a result of these changes, for nothing is lost that is worth keeping, and what is gained is immeasurable and everlasting.

As a result of becoming involved in this work, it is not uncommon for relationships, not only with spouses but with friends and entire social groups, to change. There are many people who will simply not accept what you are doing—even those who have in the past been very close to you. There is not much that you can do about the negative reactions of others except help them to see that what you are doing is right for you and that you carry no ill will toward them for not supporting you. Others will simply not understand the changes they see in you, for their own consciousness may not have changed in accordance with yours. Those who are operating on a different level of consciousness cannot experience life the way you may now be experiencing it, and you will have to find others whose states are more similar to your own. Rest assured that there will be others coming into your life who will be more suitable companions for you.

There are instances when even your spouse cannot take this next step with you. It is difficult to know if he or she will adjust to your changes without a greater perspective on these changes and the role of this individual in your life. It is possible to receive some information about this from your guide or teacher, although it is best to address this question to another medium. Usually, only general information will be offered until what to do becomes apparent to the individuals involved. Anyone capable of doing this work can trust their intuition to guide them. We trust this as well and do not interfere in this process of discovery, but there may be something we can offer that will be helpful without interfering with this choice process.

Another issue that often arises when first beginning to do this work is how your family will accept it. There will probably be as many opinions about what you are doing as there are family members. Sometimes, however, family members will band together and make demands of one sort or another. This is an excellent opportunity for the issue of who is responsible for one's life to be addressed. The answer is simple enough: Only you can live your life and meet the consequences of your decisions. If you make decisions based on what others want for you rather than on what you want for yourself, you will not be acting in accordance with what is best for your own growth. Even if your choices are less than the best, they are still yours, and in making them yourself, you will learn to make more satisfying ones. All you are likely to learn when you allow others to make choices for you is that you should have chosen for yourself. By being challenged to accept your new path, family members may learn important lessons. The experience may even open their minds to the forces in the universe beyond their senses.

HOW TO CHANNEL

Prior to the development of trance channeling, do not use a ouija board. Meditate regularly, use channeling only rarely, and do not share information you receive with others. In other words, before trance channeling develops, do not consider yourself a channel, be very skeptical about the information you receive, and focus on your spiritual development through meditation. Before trance channeling develops is when channeling can be most dangerous. More will be said about this in the next chapter. The best advice for this stage is don't channel and beware of the potential dangers if you do.

A number of conditions are necessary before trance channeling can begin. First of all, you will not be able to channel in either full or partial trance if your nervous system is not sufficiently developed. Secondly, even if it is, you may still be prohibited from trance channeling by your Higher Self if you are not ready in other areas of your development. Thirdly, you may be ready in every way developmentally, but the proper time in your life may not have arrived. And finally, the proper time may have arrived, but the specific circumstances in your life may not be supportive, and you may need to wait a short while until the right circumstances emerge.

If you have the potential for trance channeling but you are being prohibited from doing it for any reason, you must simply wait until that prohibition is lifted. It is easy enough to know when that is, because you will simply not be able to channel in trance before this time. However, it is preferable to wait until a reliable teacher or guide notifies you rather than attempting it periodically yourself, because your attempts are likely to attract lower astral beings. They cannot enter or harm you in any way, but it does not serve them or yourself to put out this message of openness indiscriminately. The desire to channel in trance may, in fact, be what must be overcome; your motives must always be examined. Many waste time and energy attempting to channel before they are ready, and many are never ready. You must live in the assurance that if this is to be your work, it will unfold naturally and without your pressing it.

Elaborate preparation is not needed before a fully developed channel can receive messages mentally, although channeling in trance will require the same type of preparation regardless of one's development. One who is a fully developed channel need only refrain from making strenuous or sudden motor movements or from having strong emotions in order to receive messages mentally. It is even possible to receive brief messages while showering, cooking, walking, eating, or engaging in other mild activities as long as the heart rate does not dramatically increase. Admittedly, individuals capable of this are rare, but this level of ability does exist. One word of caution here: Developing channels can receive messages from lower astral beings while engaged in various activities too. It takes very little development to channel lower astral beings even while moving. The difference is that a developing channel cannot reach beyond the lower astral while engaged in activity and a fully developed channel can.

If you are a new trance channel, having done this at most in only one previous lifetime, it may take months or even years before you are able to exit the body with ease. The most difficult thing about full trance channeling is letting go of one's consciousness. This challenge may be aggravated by the signs in your astrological chart or certain past life tendencies. Those who have a need for control will have a harder time making the transition to loss of consciousness than those who do not. If you meet with this type of problem, it is best to be gentle with yourself and know that in time this difficulty will pass. Each attempt, even if unsuccessful, will advance your progress. Although the first few experiences of exiting the body can be a struggle, after the first two or three successes, it becomes much easier. The only thing that can stand in the way of eventual success for someone who is ready is giving up.

Once you are able to channel in full trance, you have access to different levels of intelligence, and you must choose with whom you will communicate. Less developed channels will not have access to as high a level of intelligence as those who are more developed. This in no way detracts from their potential to serve, but this difference should be understood when evaluating the information received. You must always be discriminating before accepting what is offered.

When you are ready to begin trance channeling, a being usually introduces himself and asks permission to speak through you. By this time, you will be familiar with your spirit guide who is usually the one to act as a gate keeper. Your gate keeper will inform you of the level of this being, his intentions, and whether or not it is advisable for you to accept. In most cases, the being who first approaches you can be trusted to be one who has been selected for you to work with. These arrangements, or partnerships, are more often than not planned on the soul level and agreed upon some time in advance of the actual meeting. This being may be with you only a short time in order to accomplish a certain task, or he may be with you indefinitely. It is up to you to accept or reject this offer, but the usual procedure is to accept it. Asking permission is more of a rule and a formality at this point than an actual necessity for matters of safety. The fact is that once you have reached this level in your development, you will attract only those who are working in your highest good and who have similar goals to your own. Nevertheless, beings always respect the right of a channel to accept or refuse their offer.

Usually the being will introduce himself by name, although beings usually do not have names until they begin communicating with those on earth. The name sometimes has significance to the being and sometimes not. We have no need of names here, so we do not hold much importance in them. In reality we are undifferentiated from you or anything else. We differentiate only to perform our functions, after which we reintegrate with All That Is. We are in constant rapid oscillation between awareness of ourselves as All That Is and awareness of ourselves in our specific functions. It serves our function to individuate to some extent and express ourselves in some form of personality. Our former existences have shaped a personality for us, but this personality is more like a cloak that we don and remove when it suits us. We do not don various personalities for various occasions except in rare instances. Just as we have developed a personality of sorts, we also have developed goals and expertise in certain areas. What we choose to accomplish will be mostly consistent with our personality, because both one's personality and one's goals stem from one's experiences and native tendencies. Beings with whom you will be able to speak will show all types of personalities.

Because of our unique goals, some beings will be more suited to certain mediums than others. Several factors are taken into consideration before a medium is approached to share in a certain task. The most important factors are the medium's philosophy, goals, and life Plan. A basic similarity in philosophy is helpful but not necessary. If a similar philosophy is not held, much time may be needed to educate and negotiate new ideas, which in some cases may even be the main purpose for the relationship. Similar goals are perhaps the most important factor to consider in a partnership. The goals for doing this work are many: Some mediums want to work as healers, some as educators, some as information gatherers, and some simply want to work privately with a non-physical teacher. Likewise, beings may choose to be healers, spiritual teachers, personal guides, or educators. Another consideration is the medium's life Plan and how it fits with the being's Plan. Most of these partnerships—at least the long term ones—facilitate each other's Plans for the time they are together.

Many people are under the impression that grounding exercises, which include surrounding oneself with White Light, are necessary before channeling. The truth is that for all but those in the stage just prior to full trance channeling, these exercises are nearly totally ineffective, and they have very limited value even for those in this stage. Once full trance mediumship emerges, grounding and protection happen of their own accord, without the channel's direction. What is actually dangerous about these exercises is that they lead undeveloped channels to believe that performance of these exercises will protect them when, in fact, in the early stages of development there is no protection.

Grounding cannot be manufactured, it must be earned. It is a function of one's spiritual development and readiness to do this work. If you have to work at grounding, you are not ready to do this work. In a similar vein, if you have to work at developing psychically, you are not ready to be a psychic. If you are to do this kind of work, these things will come relatively easily; it will be apparent that you have already developed this gift.

Quieting of the emotions, body, and mind is needed, however, before going into full trance. Some mediums simply sit quietly and wait while others engage in some form of meditation. The more experienced the medium is in calming herself, the more quickly this preparation phase goes. When the medium is sufficiently quieted, the gate keeper will introduce the being if he is unknown to the medium, otherwise the being will simply introduce himself at that point.

Once the being has introduced himself, the channel must give him permission to speak through her. It is important to include the name in the permission you give. Beings are not allowed to enter a medium without permission, and they are not allowed to give false names. Asking for identification is a safety procedure that is the medium's responsibility. When mediums become lax in doing this, they open themselves up to lower astral beings. No harm can come of this to the medium, but she might find herself giving false information to unsuspecting listeners. This may not even be discovered by the medium in full trance unless a member of the audience recognizes the difference in voice and expression of the unexpected guest. This kind of misadventure has been known to continue for some time before discovery, but following this very simple procedure can prevent it.

After permission is granted, the full trance channel will lose consciousness. Her head is likely to be unsupported for a brief moment during entrance and exit, so support of some sort, from a high-backed chair for instance, is helpful. From this point until the being departs, the channeling session is in the hands of the being who will be able to speak and animate the features of the medium according to the being's own level of experience. Some very advanced at channeling through mediums are able to walk or pace if they choose. This can help get the message across, which is usually why it is done. When the medium returns to consciousness, she may need some time to reorientate herself and meet some of her physical needs, but all in all, this experience will have no dramatic effect on the medium except perhaps fatigue.

The procedure is basically the same for channeling in partial trance except the medium remains conscious, although very passive. There is no need to support the medium in partial trance, because her own muscles, along with some additional assistance from the being, are able to do this without interfering with the message. The challenge for the partial trance medium is also in letting go, although she does not have to let go of consciousness— only of conscious control. The fully developed and experienced partial trance medium has no difficulty remaining passive, but the newcomer to this form of channeling may have some difficulty preventing her own words from being inserted into the message. However, as explained earlier, the tendency to insert words usually poses no significant problem to the delivery of the message.

The age and physical condition of the medium will influence her capacity to channel. The stronger the nervous system, the more frequently she can channel and the longer she can sustain it. Unfortunately, age takes its toll on the nervous system, as it does on all aspects of physical functioning, so a medium's capacity will decrease with age but not necessarily her ability.

Meditation, proper sleep, and proper diet are means by which the nervous system can be strengthened. Eating leafy green vegetables and spirulina; and cutting out caffeine, sugar, alcohol, and other drugs will strengthen the nervous system, although, no amount of diet therapy can prepare your nervous system to channel if you are not ready in other respects. Deep sleep helps to restore the nervous system more so than long sleep, which may actually work against strengthening the nervous system by preventing you from sleeping deeply. If you are not getting enough deep sleep, sleeping five to six hours a night with a brief nap during the day might help.

CHAPTER V

THE SESSION

In order to have a successful experience with a channel, you as a wise consumer must actively seek a reputable channel, formulate your questions carefully, and utilize the information responsibly. The session, whether you realize it or not, is an interchange, not a one-away street. Most beings require you to structure the session with your questions, because they will not address issues of importance to you except with your permission. What you ask will determine the content of the session, and what you do with the information will determine its effect on your life. Thus you must be the shaper and determiner of your experience.

FINDING A GOOD CHANNEL

Your first responsibility, and possibly the most important, is finding a good channel. If you do not go to a reputable channel, you may receive inaccurate information, bad advise, and little help with evaluating and understanding your channeling experience. You may be flattered, scolded, told what to do, or patronized. These are all inappropriate ways for a being to relate to you, but even beings on the higher astral do these things on occasion. To add further confusion, even a good channel may mistakenly channel a lower astral being if she is lax in the preparation phase and does not request identification before channeling. A good channel can also be corrupted if she channels while overwrought or exhausted. Some channels push themselves beyond their limit, which can lead to a breakdown of their ability to reach higher levels of intelligence. It is wise to observe the kind of schedule or lifestyle the medium leads to determine whether or not she may be vulnerable to this difficulty. And because sometimes even channels with excellent reputations may deliver messages of poor quality from time to time, finding a channel with a good reputation is not a guarantee of receiving quality information. You must always evaluate each piece of information carefully. Watch for the following warning signs in the message you are receiving:

Blatant ordering, telling you what to do in a specific situation. Example: "Get out of your marriage, it is not good for you."

Flattery, compliments, exuding love in a personal sense. Example: "You are too fine a person to have to work so hard and receive so little appreciation."

Condescension, patronizing, playing the role of the Father or the All-Wise. Example: "Dear child, don't you know that all is being taken care of by those who are watching over you?"

Belittling, scolding, admonishing. Example: "It's time you understood that you are not the only one in the universe and started taking other's feelings into consideration."

Speaking in glowing terms about Love, Unity, Peace, and God without addressing your questions directly. Example: "Love is All, life is an illusion that you must simply endure."

Being a buddy or being overly jocular, friendly, or personal. Example: "If your face gets any longer, you'll have to pick it off the floor."

Use of colloquialisms, non-standard English, slang, trendy phrases. Example: "That's a piece of cake for guys like you."

Pompous language, superiority. Example: "Do ye not know that we loveth thee even when you fail?" (Not all archaic language is to be suspect, but coupled with an attitude of condescension or other warning signs, it is worth questioning.)

Statements that induce fear. Example: "Prepare yourselves, for the end of your great land as you know it is near. A great earthquake will split your nation in two, and only half the population will survive."

Specific predictions about the future. Example: "The agency with whom you interviewed will be calling you next week with a proposal for employment."

You have two choices if you suspect that you are speaking with a being who is not knowledgeable enough to be of help. First, you can address him with your suspicions by stating why you feel uncomfortable and ask him to identify himself. It is a rule that one must identify oneself accurately when working with a trance medium. If you are not familiar with the being that the medium usually channels, this approach may not be that helpful, but some beings will leave if they feel they have been found out. And, if you are still uncomfortable, we suggest you simply state this and express your desire to end the session. The medium may not be up to trying again depending on her energy level, and you will have to respect that. Even if the medium insists on continuing, it may not be worth your while if the difficulty was due to her fatigue in the first place.

If you reject the being that you are speaking with, the medium may respond in a number of ways. If she is defensive, hurt, or angry, this is something to be wary of. A good medium will be objective about her work, accepting your skepticism and the possibility that your evaluation may be valid. Even if she is convinced that the message was valid, she will respect your opinion and your response without taking personal offense. Most mediums are capable of relating to you from a level that is beyond the personality, even when their work is being questioned. Although one cannot expect mediums to be saints, emotional reactions to skepticism are a sign that the medium is invested in her work in a way that is perhaps unhealthy, and this may reflect in the quality of the message she is able to deliver.

One of the greatest difficulties with channeling as it is today is the lack of credentialing for mediums. There is nothing to prevent an individual from claiming to be a channel and charging money for this. As you can well imagine, there are opportunists who take advantage of an unregulated business such as this. Frauds, pretending to be channels, are in the vast minority, however. The credibility of this field is more threatened by 1) those who are not sufficiently developed but think they are, 2) those who are not discriminating in whom they allow to speak through them, and 3)those who through ignorance, lack of proper preparation, or fatigue fall short of delivering quality messages. The answer to the dilemma of fraud is proper licensing; the answer to ignorance about one's level of development, the level of those they speak to, and how to properly prepare to channel is education; and the answer to fatigue is, of course, rest and balance in one's life.

Licensing is certainly a difficult question. How does one license mediumship or other psychic abilities? Obviously, the licensing will have to be accomplished by other professional mediums who speak with, observe, and evaluate the medium rather than through examination or other indirect means. It will have to be performed by a group of mediums to insure fairness and consistency in evaluation, and guidelines will have to be created as the basis for evaluation.

The problems with getting a licensing program under way are two-fold: Creating an organization to do this and establishing guidelines and a procedure for doing this. This will take a number of motivated and dedicated mediums who have sufficient concern for the respectability of their profession and its future. We feel certain that there are sufficient numbers of you who are concerned enough to invest time and energy in such a project, and we encourage you to begin. Specific suggestions regarding guidelines and procedures will be forthcoming if we are asked, for we are committed to assisting in the transformation of this activity so channeling can indeed make the respectable and viable contribution to society of which it is capable.

Education of mediums is a problem, because there have not always been the resources or teachers available to new channels. Today the number of channels is increasing not only because there are more people capable of channeling, but also it has become popular. Unfortunately, available information and good teachers have not kept pace with the increasing interest, and inexperienced channels are being led by equally inexperienced and uninformed ones. Contributing to this problem is the misconception that if you can do it, then you are a channel; when in reality, it is far more complex than that.

To do channeling well takes a degree of understanding and spiritual development few possess. The proper attitude is as important as any amount of skill or education one might have. It cannot be attained overnight but takes lifetime upon lifetime to develop. Training and education are helpful, but only in so much as they are likely to weed out those who are not yet ready. No amount of training or study can prepare someone who does not already have the necessary spiritual development.

Some individuals, having chosen to concentrate on the development of this ability over a number of lifetimes, may be able to channel but may not have the necessary spiritual development. This is a dangerous situation. When the ego is involved, one's ability to discriminate and to be objective is lessened. But more importantly, it is easy for channels such as this to abuse their power and attract beings equally interested in telling others what to do because their motives are still attached to the ego. Like attracts like, and one can judge a medium by the company she keeps. Individuals who are capable of channeling but who are not developed spiritually will attract lessons that will right the imbalance created by their uneven development. These lessons can be painful to the channel and equally painful to the followers who also undoubtedly attracted this experience to learn about power. Individuals who abuse power in this way are likely to find themselves without it and with virtually no more credibility. Those who fall from such positions fall hard.

Education is need to weed out those who are not ready to do this work and to initiate those who are. Much of this can be accomplished through books, but sometimes direct contact with a teacher is needed to convince certain individuals of their lack of readiness. This can be accomplished easily enough in a session with a medium, although a good medium, herself, is likely to have a very good sense of whether an individual is ready or not.

Those who are ready need support from others who are doing this work. This has not always been available, and it is one reason for beginning a licensing organization, which could also serve as a support network. Most individuals who are ready to do this work do not need information, which they can receive from their guides, as much as they need support. Becoming a medium changes one's life in nearly every respect. Other mediums are able to meet each other as equals, which is not always possible with people due to their projections. Mediums are also able to act as foils for each other, spotting each other's weaknesses and offering objective opinions. Because mediums can lose their objectivity and their ability over time, they need others who will be honest with them about what they see happening. Thus an organization would serve not only to initiate members into this work but support and evaluate them on an ongoing basis.

FORMULATING YOUR QUESTIONS

After selecting a medium, the next area of responsibility for the consumer is formulating questions. It is not that poor questions will preclude receiving any benefit from a session, because the being you are speaking with will steer you in other more appropriate directions if need be; but time is limited, and it might as will be used efficiently. **How you ask the questions will influence the responses you get.** For instance, if you ask, "Will I be able to find a job soon?" the answer will be structured around when you will find a job. The trouble with this is that it is too narrow a question and too difficult to answer with any accuracy. It also may not address the root of the problem, which may be more along the lines of, "What kind of work am I best suited for?"

The first rule in formulating questions is: **Ask open-ended questions—questions other than those that require a simple one or two word response.** Questions that are not open-ended limit the possibility of elaboration on the part of the being. Remember that, out of respect for your freedom of choice, you will not receive information that you do not request. Consequently, you are likely to gain far more from a reading if you construct your questions in a way that will give the being permission to answer more elaborately.

The most useful beginning words to use to insure that a question is open-ended are "what" and "how." Questions that begin with "when," "who," and "where" may be asked, but they will give you short answers at best. For the most part, however, these questions are not appropriate because their answers are too specific and either cannot be known or it will not be in your best interest to know them. There is always a deeper question behind questions beginning with "when," "who," and "where," which is the one that needs to be addressed. It is best to rephrase such questions to begin with "what" or "how."

The future is the least fruitful area of inquiry. Questions pertaining to the future will only be answered in very general terms. It is best to phrase them very generally, too, and to understand that the answers may change with time. Answers to questions regarding the future are based for the most part on the probable future that is being created by the present actions of the individual, which can change at any moment. It is true that sometimes events are preordained by the soul, but it is never certain when a preordained event will manifest, because it must be woven into the context already created by the individual's choices. Besides, these preordained events are few and far between, and they are almost never revealed to the individual beforehand. It would serve no purpose to do so and might hinder the natural course of events set in motion by the individual's choices. Thus the only information you are likely to receive about the future will pertain to the probable future you are creating, and you can predict this yourself to some extent. At best, the being may be able to add something very general that may also enter into the situation. The second rule in formulating questions is: **Avoid expectations of receiving specific information about the future, and understand that information you do receive may change over time.**

Another area of inquiry where expectations run high is past lives. Although exploring aspects of your past lives can have great value and relevancy, a word of caution is in order here. Not only is past life information difficult to supply, but people are too often sidetracked from the real issues by these types of questions. Mistakenly, many look for glamour in past associations and accomplishments. This is a waste of time, and most beings will not cater to this if that seems to be the motive. Past life information that sheds light on the origin of current psychological issues and patterns is the most useful. Dates, names, places, even occupations or gender are often not needed to accomplish this goal. On the other hand, there are times when these specifics are appropriate and helpful. The third rule in formulating questions is: **Examine your motives for seeking past life information and let a desire for understanding of current issues be your guide**.

Appropriate areas for investigation are relationships, health, work, life task, and lessons. Let us look at some of these areas to illustrate the kind of information that can be received.

Everyone has relationships of various types—with friends, co-workers, lovers, neighbors, family, and others in the community. Some relationships are by choice, while others are not. We cannot always control who enters and leaves our lives, but we can be certain that life will present us with a variety of individuals who will help us grow. The relationships that are not by choice—family and co-workers in particular—offer the greatest potential for growth in their diversity and challenge. Life throws us into the ring with individuals of various levels of development, understanding, and ability, and challenges us to function along side them in harmony. This is not always easy, but it is always interesting.

Every relationship in life holds its own special lessons, and these can be elucidated to some extent in a channeled reading. We do not give away answers but supply just enough information to feed your imagination about the potential of any given relationship. It is important not to tell you how to see another individual, but we can give you some clues about the reason for your relationship, whether it is to learn a specific lesson or to accomplish a certain task.

We are also able to supply information regarding the dynamics of a relationship. Every person is unique, as represented in the energy map known as the astrological chart; and certain energy patterns will combine more harmoniously than others. There are also other esoteric factors that can create harmony or disharmony between two people. The picture is complicated by the fact that it is possible to get along well in some areas but not in others. Human beings are complex, and relationships are all the more so.

We are also able to provide information concerning the kind of relationship you may have had with another in former lives. The number of lives shared with another will certainly be significant in terms of how you currently experience each other. Individuals choose to re-encounter each other for various reasons: To fulfill a life task, to learn certain lessons, to repay a debt, or to develop greater love. The bond in these kinds of relationships is usually obvious to those involved, especially between individuals who meet in order to repay a karmic debt, which is often the most difficult kind of relationship. We are able to speak in general terms about the karmic circumstances and the lesson if there is one, but we rarely give specifics about either of these, because this would either serve no purpose or cause a negative effect. One of the specifics we often withhold is who is the debtor and who is the one owed, although this is usually rather apparent to those involved.

We also offer suggestions for improving a relationship without spelling out specifically what to do in certain circumstances. We are always asked about commitment. Each situation is different, and giving general advise is always dangerous. There are instances when staying with someone in spite of a bad situation would facilitate one's growth more than leaving, and there are situations in which just the opposite is true. You must try to uncover the truth about a situation intuitively, for it is your lesson. However, we are usually able to provide some information or lead you to better clarity within yourself about it.

Everyone has a life task. A life task is a general task selected for that particular life. It usually involves the development of a talent or the completion of some goal that is in keeping with other talents or goals in previous lives. We are only able to describe your life task very generally, because it is usually not predetermined and it must be shaped by your choices, although we can offer advise about it when asked.

The life task is sometimes the same as one's work, but not necessarily. If you have questions about your work or about how your life task relates or does not relate to it, we are able to address these. Often, work on the life task does not even begin until one's later years, so occupations necessary for support may have nothing to do with it. But one's occupation, regardless of whether it involves the life task, is always an important area of learning. In a reading we are able to give you a perspective on your work and how it fits into the overall scheme of your life. Some jobs lead to something else in the future, serving as stepping stones to more complex or more fulfilling tasks; while others help us grow interpersonally, develop a specific skill, or gain a particular understanding. When the objective is fulfilled, one usually feels a restlessness. If you have a reading at such a point, we will be able to offer encouragement to act on your feelings, if that appears to be in your highest good, and provide some general direction or clarity in regards to the next step.

In addition to a life task, everyone also chooses certain lessons prior to entering the body. The lessons may involve basic life lessons necessary to all human evolution, a karmic debt, or the release of a negative psychological pattern. Whatever the lesson, most are aware of its operation in their lives to some extent. When given the opportunity, we will elaborate on any lessons referred to in a reading. If someone does not ask questions about these lessons, we may even ask them if they would like to hear something about a certain one. If the reading has been entered into only out of curiosity, they may decline. It is not uncommon for this to happen, and if little interest in true growth is evident, we do not press the issue. It is important to understand, though, that you will get out of a reading only what you are willing to receive. Also, please realize that your attitude influences whether you perceive the information as valuable or not; whereas, we always perceive it so, or we would not deliver it.

WHAT TO DO WITH THE INFORMATION

What you do with the information you receive often depends on what your needs were in seeking it. If you were looking for someone to tell you what to do, you may perceive that this was done, make a choice, and assume that the decision was made for you by the reading. On the other hand, if you perceived that the reading did not tell you what to do but you wanted it to, you may disregard the entire reading. The fact is that there are few individuals who hear the reading as it was meant to be heard. One's needs invariably interfere with hearing the message as it is simply and generally stated. The tendency is to read something into the message, assuming it said something it did not, and carry on on the basis of this assumption. This is no reason to disregard channeled material, which when handled properly, can yield useful information, encouragement, and understanding. But this tendency does necessitate looking very closely at how you handle it.

When it comes to channeling, the subject of responsibility always arises. Who is responsible for what? From our point of view, everyone involved is responsible for a different aspect of the channeling experience. The non-physical teacher and the channel are responsible for providing accurate and appropriate information in a comprehensible and sensitive fashion. The receiver is responsible for requesting it, hearing it, asking for further clarification if need be, and responding to it. The non-physical teacher cannot control what happens to the information beyond the session, because he cannot communicate with the receiver unless the receiver initiates it. Thus another responsibility of the receiver may to arrange another session to check his progress. When left to one's own devices, more often than not, some misuse of the information occurs. Because of this, regular access to the non-physical teacher would be ideal. There is a need for re-structuring the channeling format to include ongoing contact rather than the once-in-a-lifetime arrangement that usually exists. Difficulties arise from this occasional format, which we encourage those in the field to remedy.

One suggestion we have for remedying this difficulty is to periodically hold small gatherings to answer the group's questions. Ideally, the group should be composed of the same individuals each time— preferably those who are comfortable with each other. There should be a fee charged for such a group if the medium is dependent on her skill for support, but at least the fee would be more manageable for a group session than that for an individual session. Another advantage of this format is that it helps to dissipate the feelings of awe that often accompany channeling. Most of all, it provides an opportunity for the members to be taught the proper relationship to channeling and to channeled information.

Unfortunately, a following sometimes develops when groups of this nature meet regularly, resulting in some of the abuses we have described. When this occurs, it is usually because members are not being confronted about their behavior by the being, the medium, or others in the group. Not all beings will educate those listening about channeling and the proper use of channeled material. Some beings do not see this as their duty, and others of a lower nature may even foster the abuse. We feel very strongly that it is the responsibility of the being to educate the listeners on these matters, and we are working to instigate more responsible behavior on the part of those in these realms. Hopefully, this book will help groups who are not being guided responsibly to use channeled information wisely.

The potential for misuse of material is lessened by the fact that information most likely to be mishandled, in the opinion of the being offering it, will not even be offered. Channeled information is given within the context of the needs of that moment; information offered under one circumstance may not be offered under other circumstances. Some people are confused by this and wonder what kind of information is appropriate to receive and what is not. Each situation is unique. The decision to offer information on any subject is based on many factors, most importantly, the being's own judgment about what effect it will have at the time it is requested. You will not receive information if it is not deemed in your best interest to receive it at that time. Nevertheless, the potential remains for misuse of the information that is offered. What follows are some guideposts regarding what to do and what not to do with the information you receive.

The first rule in handling channeled information properly is: **Do not read specifics into it**. Understand that the wording of every message is carefully chosen to be non-specific and to allow for the will of the individual to operate freely. The truth is, the specifics of a situation are not set but are created by the individual; therefore, there is no one right choice to make in any situation. Many are under the assumption that a specific plan exists and that they must simply discover it and make the *right* choices. There are no right choices and there is no *specific* plan. We cannot emphasize this enough. This is the misconception that creates the most confusion in seeking spiritual guidance. Many assume that if they could just find answers, their lives would run smoothly; but there are no answers, and the purpose of life is not ease but growth.

Growth involves making choices, experiencing their results, and making new ones based on what was learned. The life Plan that people assume to be specific is so general as to be fairly meaningless in terms of making day-to-day decisions. This Plan is helpful in understanding the context within which one makes decisions, but the myriad decisions of daily life must be made without specific outside guidance, because there is no one correct decision to make. All choices lead to learning, so it is only important that the choice you make be yours and that you learn from it.

Another useful rule is: **Never change a decision or make a decision based solely on information received through channeling**. Information is usually worded so as not to suggest a specific decision on the matter in question. However, this does not prevent someone from reading something into a response and coming to his own conclusions about a specific choice. Just remember you are the one, who must live with the consequences of your decisions, so be sure that you do not make decisions that you cannot live comfortably with— and realize that *you* are making the decisions.

Do not use the information as justification for your actions. Taking full responsibility for your actions means acknowledging your choice in the matter. Some people find it convenient to say, for example, that they left their marriage or changed their job because a reading told them to. If that is really the case, they have clearly given their power away. If it is not, they need to take responsibility for their decision. Issues can become greatly muddied by this kind of behavior, resulting in denial of the real issues.

Question yourself to find out what it is you are seeking by bringing your queries to a medium. Are you looking for information about a particular topic? help in making a decision? encouragement? advice? insight into past patterns of behavior? Or, do you want to feel superior to another? find out if you are "right" about something? be told what to do? Knowing why you are seeking information will help you determine if you are likely to misuse it once you have it. For instance, let us suppose you are looking for information about a particular relationship in your life that troubles you. Ask yourself what you will do with it once you have it. Will you use it to try to persuade your friend to see things your way or to relate to you in a certain way? Or will you use it to understand your relationship better so that you can make adjustments that will improve it? **Be clear about your motives for seeking information. If your motives are not pure, do not even ask the question.**

It is also important to note your intuitive and emotional reactions to the material after you receive it. Did it feel just right, confirming what you thought was true? Did it take you aback, making you question your current path? Did you feel awestruck by the experience? Angry? Relieved? Pleased? Skeptical? All of these are important questions, for you and your intuition are the ultimate test of the material. Being aware of how it affects you is the first step in handling it wisely. Information received from a channel should never shock or frighten you; if it does, its source should be seriously questioned. However, even information from a very reputable source may have a somewhat stunning effect. It is not unusual for individuals to seek a reading when they are confused or have lost their way, and information may serve to set them back on course. When this is the case, the information may bring about a rather dramatic realization. That is fine; some internal changes and adjustments are to be expected. However, you must carefully evaluate any actions you choose based on this realization. You must realize that a change in perception does not necessitate a change in lifestyle or any other major change. Also, be very careful not to assume that the being who delivered the understanding is advocating any one course of action.

The warning here is: **Be aware of your reactions to the material and allow some time to pass before taking any steps based on this experience.** Be wary if your response to a reading resembles a "conversion experience." Sometimes the luminous nature of the experience interferes with one's ability to evaluate the material realistically and utilize it responsibly in one's life.

Some individuals become dependent on readings because they enjoy the encouragement they receive. They would rather use readings to obtain the support they are looking for than take the harder route of asking others for what they need. In some cases, they are just looking for an easy way to feel good. These people will have to learn to get the support and recognition they crave through their own accomplishments, rather than through us. When we see this happening, we try not to short-circuit their learning process by offering them easily obtained good feelings; and if it seems that this kind of dependency is developing we will address it. The point is that channeling should not be used as a supportive relationship in your life. Thus another word of caution is: **Do not rely on channeling to meet personal needs that are best met through other types of relationships**.

Another suggestion to insure proper use of the material is not to give the message too much weight. After all, it is just information; it is not the voice of God. There is something about the experience of channeling that inspires awe in many—especially during their first encounters. Even some experienced channels may find it difficult to move beyond these feelings into a relationship. A useful guideline is: **Regard the information as if it came from a wise and trusted friend, not from God**. Information is information, whether it comes from channeling, a friend, a book, or an authority. Information, regardless of its source, must be evaluated for its veracity and applicability in your life. What is true in general or true for someone else may not be true for you. No one knows what is best for you better than you do. Besides, beings who offer information or advice sometimes make mistakes in judgment or in reading the ethers. You are the one who has to live with the choices you make, so be sure that these choices are based only on information which intuitively resonates with what you feel to be in your highest good. Channeling is a tool for receiving information, and as with any tool, you must use it wisely to benefit from it.

A SAMPLE SESSION

The following is an example of a session that was handled appropriately by both the non-physical teacher and the client. The client came prepared with questions that were general and open-ended enough to allow the entity to address the areas of concern as they saw fit.

CLIENT: What is the nature of the karma, if there is any, between my husband, (full name is given), and myself?

CHANNEL: It appears that there has indeed been a relationship in past lifetimes between "X" and yourself, although we would not term it karmic in the sense that a debt exists between you. It would be more appropriate to understand this current relationship as one that is freely chosen by both of you to grow in love for each other.

CLIENT: What are we learning by being together in this life?

CHANNEL: You are learning to love more deeply through this experience of personal love. The purpose of life is to grow in love—for one another, for all creatures, and for all of life—and it is through personal love of one other that the greatest lessons of love are learned. You and he share many common interests which serve to bind you, along with your bond from previous lives, but there are ways in which it is difficult for you to meet each other's needs. The abrasions between you are largely in the category of your differing emotional styles. It appears that you are far more apt to express yourself emotionally than he is, and this can create frustration for both of you and some lack of communication at times. At the same time, the differences between you can serve to teach each other of your different ways, so that he can learn to accommodate your needs more fully, and you, his. You are similar in terms of your soul levels, that is, you are both approximately the same soul age, which bodes well for understanding and camaraderie. Your life purposes are intertwined to some extent as well, linking your personal goal of love with another goal related to what you have come here to accomplish.

CLIENT: And what is that? What have we come here to accomplish?

CHANNEL: There is a need to involve yourselves in tasks that serve others in some way. You are both dedicated to service of some sort, are you not?

CLIENT: Yes, we are.

CHANNEL: And what specifically, may we ask, is the work you are doing at this time?

CLIENT: We are both teachers. He is a high school teacher, and I teach elementary school.

CHANNEL: And you enjoy this work?

CLIENT: Yes, most of the time, but I'm feeling discouraged about the problems in the school system with large classes, little teacher autonomy, and things like that.

CHANNEL: And your husband, is he content in his work?

CLIENT: Yes, more so than I am.

CHANNEL: It is important for you to appreciate the fine work that you are doing with youngsters in spite of the limitations. We think that in the future you will find a way to reconcile these feelings and continue on in this field in a more fulfilling way. Have you thought about working with school boards and parents groups to make the changes you would like to see in the system?

CLIENT: Yes, as a matter of fact, I've been taking my frustrations to the principal and he's suggested discussing them with the school board at the upcoming meeting.

CHANNEL: You have the capability of making an impact in your field and in your community. Continue to follow your own intuition about your work, for this is one aspect of your life task which is beginning to be more apparent in your life.

CLIENT: So, my life task involves improving education in some way?

CHANNEL: Yes, and improving some other areas that pertain to society's functioning more smoothly, efficiently, and for the good of all. Allow your feelings to guide you in becoming involved in your community and in those groups that have an effect on the welfare of the community.

CLIENT: And what about my husband's life task?

CHANNEL: It is similar to yours in that his also involves working towards improving the lives of those living in your community— both its children and its adult members. You can serve as supports for each other in these areas.

CLIENT: Thank you. I would like to have some insight into my relationship with my mother, it's always been a difficult one for me.

CHANNEL: Yes, of course. What is you mother's name? (full name is given). We see that she is someone with whom you have shared a past life— more than one. You have been together as mother and daughter before, and this is a continuation of a former experience in these roles. You have chosen to continue this experience in order to gain greater understanding about the relationship between mother and daughter. This is a common understanding to be gained— one that all who pass through human existences must attain. You are experiencing the daughter side of this dyad, and she, the mother. In other lives, you will experience the mother side, and she the daughter, but not necessarily with each other.

The current difficulty is due more to the disparity in your soul ages than any other factor. It would seem that you are not able to understand each other because of this. When two individuals are at very different places in their evolution they are learning different lessons and have different ways of perceiving life. This is one reason that there is so much disagreement among people; they simply do not see life the same way. There is very little you can do about this, for neither of you can change enough in one lifetime to make up for the difference. You must learn to accept each other as you are and move beyond the differences into a mutual appreciation for your individual spirits. This is, of course, easier said than done, but it is the work that must be done by you and by her in order to achieve greater comfort in your relationship. It is always helpful to drop one's expectations for a change in another, for these are more often than not unrealistic and serve to distance people rather than bring them together.

CLIENT: Do you think my husband and I will ever have children?

CHANNEL: Is that to say that you wish to have children but have so far been unable to conceive?

CLIENT: Yes, I want to know if we are capable of having children.

CHANNEL: We are not able to address this issue so specifically as to give you a direct "yes" or "no." But, allow us to say that you are not likely to have children within the next year or two, but after that there may be more openness to this. It would seem that there is some reason that your souls are prohibiting this experience at this time, and it is our guess that this prohibition will no longer be in effect in a year or two. We cannot be more specific about why this is occurring now, but be assured that it is in keeping with your highest good. This situation is likely to be remedied at some point in time.

CLIENT: I've had trouble with my skin throughout my life, with patchiness and scaling, and I was wondering if you have any suggestions about what to do about this?

CHANNEL: This condition is chronic and long-standing and will remain so to some extent throughout your life, although its severity is not likely to increase. It is karmic in origin, although we cannot specify the circumstances that are related to this condition. It has something to do with the need to develop humility and to experience one's vulnerability and lack of control over certain conditions. Its effects can be ameliorated to some extent by creams and lotions that are currently available. Retaining the moisture of the skin is of primary importance, and there are many products that will serve this purpose.

CLIENT: What do you see as the likely outcome of the current foreign policy between the Soviet Union and the United States?

CHANNEL: The diplomatic relations between the two countries mentioned are likely to change dramatically in the next twenty-five years. The beginnings of this are already in the wind. There will be an end to the cold war and increasing peaceful relations between these two political adversaries. There will be a coming together of political viewpoints and a healing of old wounds. The countries of the world will find it necessary and increasingly advantageous to wage peace instead of war in the coming years. Arms will be set down, making room for peaceful negotiations and trade among the nations.

CLIENT: I have one last question that I'd like to pose to you. What do you see as the coming trend in education?

CHANNEL: It will be some time before necessary reforms take hold in ways that significantly change the face of the educational system in your country. For one thing, sufficient funds are not being allocated to the education of your children. This will have to be the first step taken in bringing reform to this system. In many ways, the educational system is failing your youth. It is not addressing the current needs of the young. Their emotional needs need to be addressed within the school system as well as their intellectual needs. There is a sorrowful lack of attention paid to the whole child. Hopefully, the trend will be away from compartmentalization towards holism. There are many individuals who are working to restructure education to include other aspects of one's being, particularly the emotional and spiritual elements, which have been missing from your system. How long it will take before this becomes accepted educational policy remains to be seen, but we do believe the coming trend is toward holistic education and away from spoon-feeding children information that has little relevance to their daily lives.

CLIENT: Thank you.

CHANNEL: You are most welcome. We are pleased to be of assistance. Good night.

CHAPTER VI

CONCLUSION:

OUR MESSAGE TO EARTH

The earth is going through a transition period in which her vibrational level is being raised from third density to fourth density. What this means is that all creatures and all life forms existing within her vibrational form will need to accelerate their vibrational frequencies as well. This is coming about by various means: Some souls are leaving the earth never to return to this reincarnational system. They will go to another system whose vibration is similar to their own, and others are transforming their own vibrational frequencies to match the earth's. There are many highly developed souls who have come into the earth's reincarnational system to assist with this process. They are working to accelerate the vibrational frequencies of those currently living in a number of ways, especially through the healing professions. They are also found in the field of nutrition and in the environmental movement, working to improve overall nutrition and the nutritional value of the food you eat.

We have every reason to believe that the needs of the earth shall be met so that global disaster does not befall the earth and her people. We have this confidence in part because of the vast number of souls who have chosen to reincarnate at this time and who have come from vast distances— from other solar systems— to do so. We also believe in the capability of the human race to right the mistakes that have been made. We also feel confident because of the excellent example your country, the United States, sets for the rest of the world in its democratic political system. Democracy, in spite of its flaws, allows for the potentials of its people to be developed; and although free enterprise, which is a part of this democratic system, is partially responsible for many of the current problems, the freedom allowed by this system will also be responsible for the solutions. Ultimately, the vast human potential your democratic system fosters will set the earth back on course with a new set of values and a new understanding and appreciation for the planet you inhabit.

The course of human history is not unlike the course of the individual's evolution, for unwise choices are sometimes made and the consequences must be lived with until new and better choices bear their fruits. Whole generations of individuals will sometimes have to live with the fruits of some poor choices, but in the long range of human history, learning is accomplished and some of the same mistakes are not repeated. Just as we must have faith in the potential of the individual to learn the lessons required of him, so we must have faith in the potential of the entire human race to ultimately survive with greater understanding. This does not preclude the possibility of total devastation and loss, for you have the potential of this in your hands right now, but it is not likely that this degree of devastation will be allowed to occur.

It is true that the fate of the world lies in your hands, for it is you who are alive and physically capable of saving or destroying the earth. On the other hand, you are not alone or disconnected from others who are working for the good of the earth and for the good of her inhabitants, for many like ourselves are doing their best to guide and protect the earth. What this means precisely is difficult to describe, for the workings of the universe and our role in it are not easily understood by those who see us as separate from themselves. Perhaps it would be helpful at this time to say more about who you really are and who we really are.

You have been told that we are all One, that we are all part of God or a Universal spirit, although this concept is never fully grasped by you, nor can it be. The fact that you cannot grasp this does not in any way detract from its truth. This, in fact, is perhaps the essential Truth. Let us examine this from the standpoint of evolution, so that this concept can make better sense to you. We will tell you a story that is close to the Truth, but like a myth, is more symbolic than exactly true, because language cannot contain the abstractions we are seeking to describe. Here is our creation myth.

There was no beginning nor will there be an end, but there came a time when the Godhead differentiated in order to experience the infinite possibilities inherent in Life. This differentiation was similar to the ovum making its first division subsequent to conception, for each half was identical and equal to that from which it came. Each person grew from the Godhead in this way, each containing its Creator within it and equal to It, but with its own purpose and function, which served the Creator.

The ovum continued to divide and in its division further differentiated itself, while continuing to contain its Source deeply encoded within it. When the ovum matured, it appeared to be quite distinct and separate from the Source from which it came; and in this new form, it was able to experience life in ways that it could not before it had form. The experiences it had in this form enriched the Creator who expanded in greatness as a result. Eventually, this form was shed and other forms taken on accompanied by new and wider experiences, which continued to expand the Creator and the being within the form. As the being evolved within the various forms, the being became more aware of the Source and able to experience itself as Source from time to time, until finally, the being knew itself only as Source once again, although it also knew itself as all the forms it once experienced.

The form you are now occupying on the physical plane is only one of your many physical forms, after which there will be many non-physical forms. When you are encased in the physical, you are subject to it and to the limitations created by the mind and the sensory system. You do not know yourself as spirit on a regular basis, although some of you are able to experience yourself as this a good part of the time. When you shed the physical form for the last time, a rebirth of awareness occurs in which you remember who you really are. This happens to some extent at each physical death as well, but the experience is permanent and pervading once you are done with physical incarnations. We who are beyond rebirth know this as fact; you for the most part must accept this on faith. Let it be known that we are not here out of the goodness of our hearts to help you poor floundering souls on earth. We are here doing what we do because we *are* you. We do not experience ourselves as separate from you, although we recall our previous experience of separation and understand your current perception.

We are also not in any way concerned about the course of each of your lives, of the earth, or of the universe, for that matter; we do not perceive urgency in our work, as you might expect. We are simply performing our tasks in continual accord with the Universal Plan that is set forth. It is a little as if the drama you are currently living has already been played out and known to be successful. In fact this is precisely our experience. The future is already accomplished and the outcome known, but we are involved, nonetheless, in the ongoing drama with full knowledge of the outcome and the perfection of the Plan.

You are still creating the drama with every choice you make, but the drama that you are creating is already known to us. Thus your life appears to be made up of past, present, and future, but to us there is no dissection of time into these categories. All events could be said to have already occurred, yet they are all continually occurring. These concepts cannot be explained adequately nor understood by you, although for centuries you have tried to do so.

The universe is filled with those like yourselves who are evolving on the physical plane and those like ourselves who are evolving on non-physical planes. The universe is infinite, and the life forms that inhabit the universe are infinite and beyond imagination in their diversity. Some of you have even come from other places in the universe to experience the shift that is occurring on the beloved planet earth. The earth has a special role to play in the cosmos, even as the most infinitesimal and seemingly insignificant speck of matter does. There is nothing out of place in the universe, nothing that is going to waste, and nothing that is permanently removed from life. The universe is constantly expanding and working in absolute balance with everything that is contained within it.

There are Beings who oversee the entire functioning of the universe and help to maintain this balance. These are not beings as you might imagine, but highly evolved energy sources, so powerful and omnipresent that we stand in complete awe of their mightiness. We are able to sense their presence and respond intuitively to their energy, but we cannot communicate directly with them as we are doing now with you. In their vast proportion, they are to us as your mythical God is to you, although there are energy sources beyond them and beyond them and so on; there is no end to God. God cannot be contained within any one energy source, for God is the Source of all energy sources, yet One with every creation.

The role that your planet, earth, plays in the scheme of things is that of providing an environment in which physical life can evolve. Reincarnation through the physical plane is significant to every form of life, and nearly every form of life has at one time participated in physical plane existence. The physical plane existence lessons are like no other, and they cannot be accomplished in any other way. The conditions necessary to produce and sustain physical life are highly specific and narrow in range.

Maintenance of these conditions is one of our purposes and the purpose of many like ourselves. We oversee planets such as your own with knowledge and appreciation for the delicacy of the conditions required to sustain life, and with the deepest respect for the importance of the opportunity a planet such as yours allows in the evolutionary scheme. We are not able to affect the earth and her climate by physical means, for we have no physical means, but we are able to intuitively affect those who are making decisions that have an impact on the balance that must be maintained. Thus we are working as best we can, in concert with thousands like ourselves, to affect positively those individuals who are influencing the delicate balance which sustains life on your planet. You might be wondering how well we are doing with this task. It appears we are winning the race against time created by your technology, and that earth will eventually heal herself and return to the balance she once knew, but it will take several hundred years before the wrongs will be entirely set right.

People like yourselves have more power than you ever imagine to affect earth and the course of history. You are history; it is in your hands— each individual's hands. Know this and handle the power entrusted in you with respect. By impacting on earth, you are impacting on the entire universe. The loss of earth as a planet that can sustain life would affect the balance in the entire universe.

Some of you believe in evil forces that are working to destroy earth just as we are working to preserve it. Let it be understood that anything that could be considered "evil" by your standards is no match for the power which exists as a positive source for good. There are those who are upsetting the balance, not so much because they intend to do this, but because they have other selfish motives that cause the balance to be upset. Just as your technology did not intend to disturb the balance on this planet but it did so due to greed and short-sightedness, those working contrary to our goals are not intending to create pain. They are only trying to meet their own goals, but their goals are not broad enough to include the needs of others.

These individuals are aptly known by some as "service to self." They have taken the path of service to self as a means of evolving rather than the path of service to others. They do evolve, in a different fashion, and their evolution is focused on self-development rather than on the attainment of greater love. Eventually, their evolution will be halted along this path, and they will shift to a path of service to others, for one can only progress so far on the path of service to self. Because they are in the minority, they do not present a threat to the universe, although they are having some impact on the work we are trying to accomplish on your planet.

They are working against us primarily by instilling fear in people and reinforcing the general belief in evil. This belief in evil is partially responsible for the lack of openness to those like ourselves who are attempting to communicate directly to people on earth; the idea that we are somehow related to the Devil keeps people from hearing our message. Meanwhile, in many ways, they are acting like people suppose the Devil would act. Instilling fear is the first step in their plan to gain some control over those who inhabit the planet. They hope to eventually make the earth a station for themselves on which to base their activities in this part of the universe. This may sound far-fetched to you; nevertheless, an understanding of this is needed to dissipate their power and promote understanding.

Our purpose is not to focus on these individuals, for their impact on the course of the planet earth is minimal, although they may not wish to see it this way. What is important is that you are not alone in this vast universe; you are far from alone. There are many other civilizations like yours who are struggling with maintaining the same balance between technology and ecology. What you have created in your civilization is far from unique, for the human species— and there exist other human species in our universe— is prone to these kinds of abuses. There are many human civilizations however, who have never developed technology, yet who have evolved into highly developed and realized individuals. Technology is not a prerequisite to higher consciousness. In fact, it has often hindered the development of higher consciousness rather than facilitated it. Technology is neither solely hindering nor solely facilitating higher consciousness in your instance. There are those who are better able to achieve their potentials because technology has provided the ease to do so; and there are also those who miss the essence of life due to the distractions of technology and the fast pace of living it produces.

There are also civilizations that are non-human but physical, which follow a completely different evolutionary track than humans. The variety of these non-human physical forms is infinite, encompassing anything that can be imagined. Although humans and non-humans evolve from different reincarnational systems, ultimately the differences become non-existent as they reunite into more and more complex life forms. We, as entities, are products of the reincarnational system which includes only humans; but on levels of existence beyond our own, we combine with others from other reincarnational systems— human and non-human— to make up energies that are beyond the scope of our understanding. This combining of energies continues infinitely, and the Godhead is continually expanding into infinity as a result of these combinations.

Normally, you are not able to communicate with or perceive those who are non-physical, but conceivably you could perceive any physical form, human or non-human. When your technology reaches the point of being able to extend to distant corners of the universe, you will encounter some of these other human and non-human physical forms, if they do not come to you first. Currently, monitoring your civilization are non-physical beings imperceptible to most and some simple machines or stations similar to those you are sending out into space. To our knowledge, there are currently no physical beings seeking to make contact with you or walking among you in disguise as some of you believe. This is not to say that there is not this possibility in the near future, for it is only a matter of time before you will come in contact with other civilizations like your own. Those who have considered making contact have chosen not to do so yet because they appreciate that doing so might upset the very crucial course of events of the next few years, which will usher in a new respect for the earth and a new relationship to it.

The fact that you are not alone in the universe should be a comfort to you, for the life forms that do exist are for the most part benevolent and evolved beyond that of your system. This does not mean that you are the babies of the universe, although some on your planet are. Perhaps as many as ten percent of you are actually from other planetary systems and were highly evolved before coming to this one. Those who have chosen to come here to assist the earth and her people during this time of stress and transition are sometimes called "wanderers" or "star people." We prefer to call them "helpers." This is a suitable name, because of their intent and because most come from systems in which service is practiced to the level of an art. These evolved systems have chosen to dedicate their energy to uplifting systems in the universe that are in particular need. They are like the Red Cross of the universe, if you don't mind the comparison.

Because these "helpers" are so evolved, they do not entirely fit in with those who are native to earth. They usually sense that they are different and question their existence and purpose more strongly than others. Most choose to participate in reincarnation in the usual way so that they gain the understanding and experience needed to be fully of the earth, but they move through the reincarnational plan far more quickly than those native to earth. "Helpers" who have evolved to the Old soul level are operating on a very high level, indeed, for not only have they earned this level through accomplishing the lessons, but their true state of development begins to be apparent at about this stage, although even in their earlier lifetimes their greater love, compassion, and desire to serve are apparent. By this time, they will usually also have recovered some of the psychic gifts developed in their previous lives elsewhere. In fact, most individuals who are highly developed psychically on your planet today are "helpers" who have ripened to this stage at this very crucial time in earth's history.

"Helpers" take part in all walks of life, but most commonly in the healing professions. They gravitate toward these professions, because it is through this type of work that they can accomplish the most good. Many are able to take the traditional means for healing and expand upon them, making them more effective and efficient. Many of these individuals send healing energy to people without trying and without even being aware of doing this. In spite of this, many of the new healing techniques being explored by the so-called New Age movement are only in the very beginning stages, and those working with them have only a beginner's understanding of them. These techniques are primitive by our standards and relatively ineffective, but this is no reason to discontinue their exploration. The future will see great advances in the art of healing, and many of these techniques are forerunners to later related techniques of great power and effectiveness.

The thread running through most of these new techniques is the use of the mind to heal the body. It is now accepted that the mind plays a very important role in healing. You must also come to see that individuals can heal themselves by bringing their personal selves into alignment with their spiritual selves. Many illnesses today are catalysts to opening the individual's spiritual eyes; and when this is the need, no amount of medicine, positive thinking, or other technique will suffice. Contrarily, for one who is connected to spirit, techniques are immaterial. Techniques are only helpful for those whose mental, emotional, or physical bodies are the focus of their illness; spiritual problems require spiritual solutions. If the illness or difficulty is caused by the disconnection of the individual with his spirit and the Plan set forth prior to life, he must be reconnected to it in order to become whole. This requires individuals capable of reading the soul's Plan.

Individuals most equipped to do this are psychics, astrologers, and mediums. The problem with this group of individuals is the lack of quality control among them. How does an ordinary individual, particularly one vulnerable and in pain, determine who is capable of revealing the soul's Plan and who is not? The truth is that there are not many capable of doing this. Another fact is that there are many psychics, mediums, and astrologers who believe they are capable but are not. That is perhaps the most dangerous fact. Many of these so-called professionals grasp at the power and control they are given and advise others inappropriately, causing more problems than they solve. Unfortunately, clients may be dissatisfied with someone who does not give them specific answers and may seek someone else who will "predict the future" and tell them what they want to hear.

The public must be educated about the capabilities and limitations of channels, psychics, and astrologers; and there must be some willingness on the part of the public to seek answers to their questions responsibly. Both of these things would help to avoid the fraudulent and irresponsible practices in this field, but more than this is needed. What is needed is a system of licensing for psychics, mediums, astrologers, and others acting as spiritual guides. Training under a specialist, examination, and licensing are required for other professionals working in equally important capacities. It is time that standards are set in this area as well. The existence of these abilities in some must be acknowledged so that those few who are capable of helping can get on with their work in a respectable fashion and those who are not will stop dabbling in it and find some more fitting way to serve.

Another problem with some of the new forms of healing is that they, ironically enough, are not holistic. Although they claim to be holistic, many leave out one or more of the aspects of being—body, mind, emotions, and spirit. Body-workers focus on the body and on the emotions, when in many cases, the difficulties in the body may derive from unhealthy mental attitudes. Psychotherapists work with the emotions and the mind and sometimes with the body, leaving out the spirit, although more are including this. Those who work with crystals, stones, pyramids, and other energy magnifying devises may not be properly attuned to the spiritual needs of the individual, and may direct energy inappropriately. These particular methods are also at a very primitive stage of development, and even in the best hands, have little effectiveness. Herbal and nutritional healing play an important role in healing the physical body, but it is only one aspect of the self and usually represents the symptoms of disease rather than the cause.

Each method of healing must begin with the cause, and this is not easily determined without spiritual understanding. A nutritionist will look for the cause in diet; a body-worker, in stress or emotional trauma; and a psychotherapist, in the early childhood. These disciplines must open up to each other and begin to work together to facilitate the integration of the whole person, but the healing process must begin with the determination of the reason for the problem. This is where psychics and mediums come in. Good ones are able to identify the starting place from which healing must proceed, and from this point the other healers must work in concert.

Another area that needs reform in outlook is your attitude toward the environment. Your civilization need not give up its comforts and conveniences to regain the natural order on earth; you need only develop new, more responsible ways of achieving these comforts and conveniences. Your scientists are working on new ways of providing fuel and other products you desire without damaging the environment, but total commitment to this has yet to be made. Your government is dragging its feet in support of what needs to be done in deference to all the special interest groups that might be affected by these changes. Progress must not be halted because of short-term consequences. Change is a part of life, and those affected by these changes will have to adapt. This is not being insensitive, merely realistic. Many are working with chemicals and nuclear energy. They endanger their health as well as the environment's, and they would be better off finding other means of support.

Protecting the environment is a global concern and cause for global steps. It is becoming obvious that everyone on earth is in this together and needs to pull together in order to solve these problems. Grappling with these problems will take you one step further along the road to world unity, which we see as the key to a new Golden Age on your planet. There are a number of steps that need to be taken before this age can come into being, but some of you will see the beginnings of it in your lifetime. World unity is also being facilitated by your mutual trade dependencies, also a result of the depletion of the earth's resources. After all, how can you be at war with someone you are dependent upon?

The times that are upon us are times of death and rebirth in which the old order must make way for the new. Certain environmental catastrophes are likely to occur, which will not only serve to lessen the population (a major cause or aggravation of current problems) but heighten awareness that you are all one people and one planet. This is already happening to some extent, as we see countries reaching out to their former enemies with medical supplies and good will in their time of need. These calamities will also work toward greater unity and compassion for all the peoples of earth. Thus with each calamity, new understanding, awareness, and compassion are born, which represents the Higher purpose for these things.

Some of the natural disasters that will occur will be due to the natural shift in the earth's vibration and its results on the topography of earth. Other disasters will be brought about by the misuse of the earth's resources: Nuclear disasters, oil spills, and weather changes due to ozone depletion. One of the most devastating effects of humankind's shortsightedness, greed, and poverty is the destruction of the rain forests, which if allowed to continue will mean the end of life on earth. We have every confidence that this will not be allowed to continue and that the significance of what is occurring in these rain forests will bring a new awareness and reawakening of human values to the planet—before it is too late.

The troubles facing you are the fruits of your own choices, but these troubles are likely to bring about the change in awareness needed to transform your relationship with earth. Sometimes it takes losing what is dearest to you to appreciate its value, and in this case, you are coming close to losing those things most crucial to your own survival. This is bringing about a resurgence of love and appreciation for earth and her bounty. Change or perish is clearly the message of these times.

Whether you can make the necessary changes in time is the question. Those of us who are in a position to observe your dilemma have varying viewpoints, but for the most part feel confident that you and earth will survive these times. The only question that remains is how many lives will be lost and how long will it take for earth to recover from what has been set in motion by you. On this the opinions differ greatly. Some are more pessimistic than others, claiming that the solutions are too little and too late to see any kind of recovery in your lifetimes. Perhaps in another fifty to one-hundred years the earth may begin to replenish her oceans and her forests and regain some of her lost purity. Meanwhile, you will have to live with the pollution you have created and that which is to come— and so will your children. This is not altogether a healthful situation, especially for those of you with greater sensitivities.

The conditions resulting from your polluting ways will have long-range effects on your health, vitality, longevity— and the health of your children. This is perhaps the saddest fact of all, for there will be many born into your world who will simply not have the intellectual and physical potentials that you have taken for granted. Your food sources will continue to be poisoned for some time to come, and children being raised on tainted food and food lacking in nutrition will suffer. There is nothing you can do for these children; it is too late for that. But it is possible for you to make amends for future generations.

Our intent is not to be harbingers of gloom, for this is not our message, but it is necessary to face the truth of the situation before adequate solutions will be sought. Many have been too busy hiding their heads in the sand when immediate action is called for. Nevertheless, we do not feel it is too late for future generations, although current suffering cannot be avoided. The solution lies in banding together and demanding that the offenses against the environment be stopped, refusing to support those who are contributing to the problem, and petitioning those in power to allocate funds for research which will uncover the replacements needed for nuclear energy, fossil fuels, chlorofluorocarbons, and a myriad of other non-biodegradable and harmful chemicals. Further research will uncover the replacements. There are clean and abundant energy sources available which will change the face of your world in more ways than one. You who are invested in the old, damaging ways must step aside and support the new methods which ultimately spell survival for you and your children.

Many question the veracity of channeled information, and rightly so— all information received in this manner should be carefully evaluated. But communications from non-physical be-ings have always been part of the human experience, and they have been responsible for many esoteric understandings, technological advances, and other new ideas. Communications from these realms come not only in the form of channeled messages but through dreams, visions, intuitive knowings, and symbols. They come through artists, priests, musicians, scientists, inventors, and ordinary men and women. What these individuals have in common is an ability to contact realms beyond the senses and bring forth new information and understanding. The fact that this occurs—that new discoveries are continually being made—means that paradigms are always in flux to some extent. Today the great influx of information is bringing about a major paradigm shift that includes a coming together of science and religion.

Religion and science are discovering that they are describing the same miraculous world but using different terminology. The energy of life, called love, that pervades everything is now visible to the eye with the help of certain instruments. The infinity of both the microcosmic and macrocosmic worlds is apparent, and the inconstancy of what you consider time and space is being made clear as well. Your scientists are more aware than ever that their paradigm is shifting and must now include concepts basic to the spiritual disciplines. Science, rather than serving to refute the paranormal as it has in the past, will be found supporting and explaining it in the not too distant future. Your present ideas about the universe and God will be seen as primitive to those in the future. Finally, science and God will be on the same side of the fence after centuries of distance, misunderstandings, and mutual disrespect. This fact alone will be the main feature of the Golden Age to come, setting it light-years apart from what you now understand. Not only will the earth be functioning on a new vibratory level, but her people will be functioning as one with a new common understanding about God and the universe.

With a common basis of understanding, much can be accomplished. So much advancement has been lost and delayed by fighting among yourselves over points of view, none of which reflected the Truth. When the Truth becomes the common understanding, it will be the basis for an entirely new order—an order based on brotherhood, peace, love, and respect for individuality and freedom. Perhaps a century will have to pass before this kind of world comes into being, but in the perspective of earth's history, this is very soon indeed. All that is occurring now is leading up to this Golden Age. You are experiencing its birthing pains.

Just what will the coming years bring? This question is cause for much speculation, and there are many different opinions. We would like to present some of our thoughts on this with the understanding that the future is not set and no one knows precisely what the next years will hold. Nevertheless, there are a number of things already set in motion that will bear fruit in the coming years which can be commented upon.

An area of concern to us is your food supply which is being threatened not only by poisoning but by extremes in weather brought about by the pollution of the environment and the destruction of the ozone layer. Famine and drought are likely to be more common as a result, with the impending loss of life. Entire countries are likely to be devastated by the results of drought, famine, and other natural disasters. Certain countries will be unable to forestall the death or overcome the total devastation that will result, and there will be little that other countries can or will do to help, because the needs will be too great. The countries most in danger of annihilation are India and some of its bordering nations and many of the African nations. These countries are already in desperate straits and cannot withstand continued famine and drought conditions. Unfortunately, in the coming years many millions of people will die as a result of famine. As ruthless as this may sound, it will eliminate some of the over-population that is troubling your planet. The souls who have chosen to enter life under these conditions have done so in full knowledge of the likely result and will accept these circumstances as part of their growth. This is not to dismiss your responsibility to help your fellow humans, but in some cases, it will simply be too late and too little. Other countries will suffer as well, but they will have the resources to continue; with the help of stronger nations, they will survive. The coming crisis on earth will draw people together as one family, for some countries will be literally saved by others.

A world government is likely to arise in response to the world crisis and to the need to regulate trade among nations. This will come about as a natural outgrowth of all that is occurring presently and will occur in the next few years. There is someone, who is now still quite young and being educated, who will lead this world government into a new international era. He is a very evolved soul who has come specifically to serve the world in this way. You will see a new kind of leadership, one that is based on true equality, brotherhood, and love for peace and for earth. In spite of what some of those of the fundamentalist persuasion have predicted about a world government and a world leader, this is perhaps one of the most positive steps humanity will take in all of earth's history. Some of you will be alive to witness this.

There will be many technological and scientific advances in the coming years that will alleviate not only ecological problems but certain shortages of materials that you are now dependent upon. It is not so much that more of these materials will be produced, but rather that alternatives to these materials will be discovered so that the current supplies need not be depleted further. Perhaps the most significant discovery in this category will be a new source of energy— or rather the harnessing of a very old source— which will be free of polluting properties. This will have the greatest impact on your transportation industry, revolutionizing it in all of its forms— land, sea, and air.

Other important advances along these lines include new cures for a variety of your ills, including cancer, AIDS, and many of the degenerative diseases such as muscular dystrophy and Alzheimer's disease. The upcoming generation will be freer of worry from many of the diseases and illnesses the current generation is suffering from, but other illnesses will appear on the scene related to immune deficiencies caused by the poisoning of your food and environment by chemicals now in use. Although use of many of the current chemicals and some of the dangerous practices will be discontinued, their deleterious effects will remain for years to come, affecting those who are being raised in the midst of the residue of these toxins. However, all in all, remarkable medical progress will be seen in the next twenty-five years. There will be some real breakthroughs in regard to the aging process and in cosmetic surgery, so you will be able to look and feel younger than your years. There will also be a resurgence of interest in proper health care, exercise, and diet, so that people will not only look and feel younger but they will live longer and more productive lives. Those of you who have not as yet begun to age measurably at this writing will undoubtedly benefit from these advances. Needless to say, greater longevity will have its impact on your social systems.

Very significant progress will also be made in space technology. More money and interest is likely to be allocated to this area once war weaponry has ceased to escalate and monopolize your resources. World peace and unity will free financial and human resources, allowing great things to be accomplished. There will probably not be actual colonization or communities in space for perhaps another one or two hundred years, for your space technology is still in its infancy. Nevertheless, your progress in this area will eventually bring to you a new perspective about yourselves, the universe, and the role you have to play in the universe.

Another area of significant advancement will be in the technology of the mind. You will learn ways to extend memory and all other capabilities of the mind, making learning simpler and more efficient. This will revolutionize your educational system; but the changes will come slowly, as they do within most institutions. In the coming times, you will find ways to maintain and advance your intellectual progress, and schools will become valued institutions of progressive thought and learning.

Another advancement that will have far-reaching effects will be the discovery of convenient and effective birth control methods.

Many of your current problems stem from your overcrowded conditions. This problem is being handled naturally through famine and death, but this need not be the case with proper education and reliable and accessible birth control methods. One stance on birth control is that it is your right to choose either to have children or not to have them, and the means to carry out this choice should be provided if it is available.

Abortion is an unfortunate attempt at birth control which will virtually become unnecessary with the discovery of new methods to prevent conception. When abortion does occur, there is some karma incurred; but it is by no means comparable to that of murder. Rather, it requires the individual to appreciate the sacredness of the act that is part of conception and the responsibility entailed in it. Because the soul does not usually enter the body of the fetus until birth or just before birth, abortion is hardly equivalent to taking the life of another, especially when it occurs very early in the pregnancy before a soul has become attached to the child. Biological life begins at conception, but life does not begin until the soul enters the body just before birth, just as it ends when the soul leaves the body. Once this understanding is made known and accepted, there will be no cause for argument.

There are other understandings that will come to light over the next few years in regard to the unseen realms and the paranormal. Science will eventually confirm and even contribute to these understandings, but initially it will be those like ourselves who will have an impact on presenting new beliefs to the public. The phenomenon of channeling is becoming more openly acknowledged and utilized, but much work remains to be done before this area is legitimized and made credible to the majority of people. There are a number of individuals who will bring to the general public new understandings and a new awareness of channeling as it is meant to be. In the future, channeling is likely to be a major vehicle for the entrance of new information and ideas into your world, and this information will affect the beliefs and perceptions of many.

One area that has not yet been touched upon is that of the social structure and, specifically, the family. Many are concerned about the current number of single-parent and broken families. This is a legitimate concern, but when placed in the proper perspective may not present so much of a problem as a temporary adjustment. The trend has been away from a family in which one parent is available to take care of the children. Consequently, many children are being raised by non-family members outside the home. This has been the fact in many societies throughout history and has worked more or less successfully.

The problems you are facing now in raising children are not so much due to their being raised by someone other than the biological mother and father, but to the low level and lack of availability of care, caused by the sudden influx of mothers into the work force. This will eventually right itself, and you will find new and better ways to raise children in groups so that they need not suffer from separation from their parents. Although there is a strong need for one-to-one attention in infancy, this attention need not only come from a parent. It is possible for children to receive what they need from those outside the immediate family if proper screening and training, and adequate pay are provided to those seeking this type of employment. There are many currently in the profession who are doing this as a last resort, for lack of any other skills. This is not an acceptable reason to be involved in child care, and this will have to change before you are able to trust your children to the child care system.

Another major social problem of your times is the lack of proper rehabilitative facilities for those convicted of crimes. This is another area, like education, where reform will come, albeit slowly. The criminal must be incarcerated *and* rehabilitated; currently, even incarceration is not being effectively carried out. More money will have to be allocated to rehabilitation and the criminal justice system, with less going to lawyers. This change will come about, but not by lawyers who are invested in maintaining their status. A similar problem exists in the medical profession, with doctors being grossly overpaid and patients being turned away for lack of financial resources. The changes in both these systems will have to come about from the taxpayers— and they will— because it will be your dollars that will continue to subsidize the high cost of crime and medicine. Consumer groups will continue to gain in strength, and the public will see that, in this democracy of yours, the people do indeed have power— if they will exercise it.

Socialized medicine is likely to be the only answer to the dilemma of high medical costs in the United States. The specific way you choose to go about this remains to be seen, but this is another important future trend that will serve to equalize some of the disparity between the wealthy and the poor in your country. It is possible for everyone to receive proper medical care, with the appropriate reforms in your medical system.

In the future, there will be some medical breakthroughs in regard to the brain and its functioning which will alleviate much of the loss of mental functioning now present in your aging population. This will allow many to live not only longer but more productive lives. With this, and proper birth control so that overpopulation is not an issue, longevity can be a boon rather than a burden to your society as it is now. People will remain in the work force longer and require fewer of your tax dollars for health maintenance. This need not prevent those who are younger from finding employment, but it is likely to influence the trend toward individuals staying in school longer. There will be a greater need for highly specialized and trained technicians, scientists, and medical personnel, and a lesser need for unskilled laborers. As you can imagine, this shift will take quite an adjustment in your educational system and many years to accomplish; but this is, nonetheless, a major future trend.

Another social trend is toward greater freedom and respect for all races and other minorities. There are a growing number of people who will simply not allow others to be treated differently on the basis of nationality, sex, race, or creed. The voices of individuals such as these were first heard in the Civil Rights movement, and they will continue to be heard. This is one trend that will not only lead to greater world unity but to greater productivity within your own country, as it is able to make use of the excellent resources offered by *all* your people.

The borders of the United States are currently being traversed by many people seeking asylum. Your country was made great by immigrants such as these who worked hard and knew the value of freedom. Once again, your country will not be marred but improved by these people who are your neighbors and who will contribute greatly to your society in the future. Please do not underestimate the potentials of these currently poor and disadvantaged people. Many great people will come from their ranks and serve your country well. They cherish the freedom and prosperity you have to offer, and they will use it well and repay you ten-fold.

We have tried to touch upon the various areas most likely to represent changes in the coming twenty or twenty-five years. For the most part, this is a general time frame, but we do see the next twenty-five years as a very important transition period in which many of your current problems will be set on fairly different courses. This is a time of great change, and times of great change require courage, fortitude, and a spiritual perspective. The spiritual perspective will be supplied by those like ourselves if asked, for we and others like us are available during these times of change for support and understanding. You are not alone.